FORTY HADEETH ON

The Call to Islam

and the Caller

Translated by
Aboo Talhah Dawood ibn Ronald Burbank

by

Shaikh 'Alee Hasan 'Alee 'Abdul Hameed

ISBN 1 898649 11 1

British Library Cataloguing in Publication Data.

A catalogue record for this book is available from the British Library.

First Edition, 1415 AH/1994 CE

Second Edition, 1415 AH/1995 CE

Printed by All Trade Printers, Birmingham, U.K.

Typeset by Al-Hidaayah Publishing & Distribution

Cover illustration by Saleem

Published by   Al-Hidaayah Publishing & Distribution

P.O. Box 3332

Birmingham

United Kingdom

B10 9AW

Tel: 0121 753 1889

Fax: 0121 753 2422

Contents

Publisher's Note

All praise is for Allaah, Lord of the worlds. Peace and blessings be upon Muhammad, his family, his Companions and all those who follow in their footsteps until the Last Day.

In the following pages we present to you an English translation of the Arabic book "Arba'oona Hadeethan fid-Da'wati wad-Du'aat," by Shaikh 'Alee Hasan 'Alee 'Abdul-Hameed al-Halabee (may Allaah protect him). The Shaikh has beautifully connected forty noble sayings of the Messenger of Allaah (ﷺ) which will, insha-Allaah, serve as an important guide for every Muslim, particularly those engaged in the field of da'wah (calling to Islaam). It will be of utmost importance to anyone wishing to implement the Prophetic methodology in the noble task of Calling to Allaah, the Most High.

Note:

> Please refer to the Arabic books for all references except where otherwise stated.

> Shaikh 'Alee's extensive hadeeth checking has been summarised to make the book more accessible for the ordinary reader.

If the reader has any suggestions for improvements in future editions then they are requested to contact the publishers.

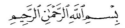

Introduction

All praise and thanks are due to Allaah, we praise and give thanks to Him, we seek His aid and ask for His forgiveness. We seek Allaah's refuge from the evil of ourselves and from our evil actions. Whomsoever Allaah guides none can misguide him, and whomsoever Allaah misguides none can guide him. I bear witness that none has the right to be worshipped except Allaah alone, having no partner, and I bear witness that Muhammad (ﷺ) is His slave and Messenger - to proceed:

This is a concise book in which I have gathered forty *ahaadeeth* from the comprehensive words of the Prophet of Allaah (ﷺ), each *hadeeth* indicating an important principle from the principles of the Call to Allaah, the Most High. Having chosen these forty *ahaadeeth,* I gathered and brought them together following the example of the scholars of *hadeeth* in gathering forty *ahaadeeth,* i.e. in a specific compilation and a particular order. I do not do this based upon what is reported in many books as the saying of the Prophet (ﷺ): **"He who preserves for my nation forty *ahaadeeth* from my Sunnah, then I will enter him into my intercession on the Day of Resurrection"** since this is a very weak *hadeeth*, all of its narrations depending upon those who are either abandoned or liars![1]

These forty *ahaadeeth* explain, in brief, the methodology (*manhaj*) of the Prophet (ﷺ) in calling to Allaah, the Most High, and that is an established and secure methodology which leaves no room for personal opinions, experimentation, or individual inclinations!

One of the major factors which lead me to compile this brief treatise was the heedless neglect by many of those who put themselves forward to give *da'wah* to the extent that you see them sanctioning many things which clearly

---

1. I have gathered many of them, and I hope that Allaah from His bounty and beneficence will enable me to put them in order and speak about them in a treatise.

conflict with the correct way laid down by the Prophet (ﷺ); and all this comes as a confirmation of his (ﷺ) saying, **"I have left you upon clear proof, its night is just like its day, no one deviates from it after me except one who is destroyed..."**[2]

"So whoever takes hold of this clear proof, and remains firm with these evidences upon the methodology of the Sharee'ah, will be safe in his *Deen* in the near and distant future. He will have clung to the firm hand-hold that will never break, and will have protected himself with a dependable shield so that he enjoys its protection, receives its blessings, and it produces an admirable result in the Hereafter and in this world if Allaah wills."[3]

I have been careful when quoting these *ahaadeeth* to provide the necessary source references and checking, following the precise and scholarly way of the People of *Hadeeth*, and in accordance with their sound method in the study of chains of narration and in passing judgement upon it (the *hadeeth* in question) as demanded by the *hadeeth* sciences - whilst trying to be brief and not going into great detail.

As regards the texts of the *ahaadeeth*, I have expended great effort in selecting them and carefully supplying chapter headings for them. I have not written down any of my own words except where that was necessary in order to connect the *ahaadeeth* like the links of a chain - each one joined to the next.

If these forty *ahaadeeth* were to be explained fully in detail then our book would become a fair-sized volume, and perhaps that will be done in the future if Allaah ordains it - if there is time in ones' life.

Finally, I do not intend by this work of mine except to show the truth, and to lead to correct guidance - and for these two goals brevity is sufficient.

---

2. Refer to *hadeeth* no. 6 for full text. Its sources are referenced there.

3. From the introduction to *Sharh Usool I'tiqaad Ahlis Sunnah* (1/10) by Imaam al-Laalikaa'ee.

So I ask Allaah to grant me success in my task, and to protect me from trials, the apparent and the hidden ones. Indeed, He is the One Who hears and responds.

And our final call is that all praise and thanks are for Allaah, the Lord of the worlds.

'Alee Hasan 'Alee 'Abdul-Hameed al-Halabee al-Atharee
11th Rajab 1408 H
(28/2/1988)
Az-Zarqaa (Jordan)

Hadeeth One
The Foundation of Actions

From 'Umar ibn al-Khattaab *(radiyallaahu 'anhu)*, who said that Allaah's Messenger (ﷺ) said:

» إِنَّمَا الأَعْمَالُ بِالنِّيَّاتِ، وإِنَّمَا لِكُلِّ امْرِىءٍ مَا نَوَى، فمن كانَتْ هجرتُهُ إلى اللهِ ورسولِهِ، فهجرتُهُ إلى اللهِ ورسولِهِ، ومَن كانت هجرتُهُ إلى دُنيا يُصِيبُها، أو إلى امْرَأةٍ يَنْكِحُها فَهِجْرَتُهُ إلى ما هاجَرَ إليهِ. «

Actions are but by intentions and there is for every person only that which he intended. So he whose migration was for Allaah and His Messenger, then his migration was for Allaah and His Messenger, and he whose migration was to attain some worldly goal or to take a woman in marriage, then his migration was for that which he migrated. [4]

This *hadeeth* establishes a very important principle from the principles and foundations of the *Deen* since the intention is the foundation for actions to the point that Aboo 'Ubaid said, "There is not, amongst the narrations from the Prophet (ﷺ) anything more comprehensive and sufficient and of greater benefit than this *hadeeth*."[5] 'Abdur-Rahmaan ibn Mahdee said, "Whoever wishes to compile a book then let him begin with this *hadeeth*."[6]

---

4. Reported by al-Bukhaaree (eng. trans. vol. 1, p.1, no. 1) and Muslim (eng. trans. vol. 3, p. 1056, no. 4692).

5. *Muntahal-Aamaal* (p. 42) of as-Suyootee.

6. Ibid.

So it is essential for the caller (*daa'ee*) to correct his intention so that he sees all the affairs in their true perspective so that they are not disguised by false adornments. When his heart is settled with this, then it will be easy for him to realize the true state of the *Ummah* today, and the humiliation which the Muslims are suffering.

Hadeeth Two
The Humiliation of the Muslims

From Ibn 'Umar *(radiyallaahu 'anhuma)* who said that Allaah's Messenger (ﷺ) said:

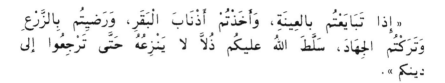

When you take part in *'eenah*[7] transactions, take hold of the tails of cows, become satisfied with cultivation and abandon *jihaad*, Allaah will send humiliation upon you and He will not remove it until you return to your Deen.[8]

The state of affairs of the *Ummah* described in this *hadeeth* is "something that we are witnessing and its signs are seen upon the Muslims, in that they have become slaves of the earth and of agriculture. Indeed this is apparent in every nation that is enslaved by the earth, which has satisfied itself with agriculture, and it is *jihaad* in Islaam which is the prerequisite for success in the affairs - whether the slaves of Europe are pleased or not."[9] This humiliation

---

7. A transaction that involves usury (interest) [Publishers' note].

8. Reported by Aboo Daawood (eng. trans. vol. 3, p. 985, no. 3455), Baihaqee (5/316) and ad-Doolaabee in *al-Kunaa* (2/65). And it is reported by Ahmad (no. 4825) and Aboo Umayyah at-Tarsoosee in *Musnad Ibn 'Umar* (no. 22).

The *hadeeth* is raised to the level of *hasan* by combination of these two chains, particularly since it has other chains of narration which we will indicate so that they can be referred to: in at-Tabaraanee's *Mu'jamul-Kabeer* (no's. 13583 and 13585), *Musnad Abee Ya'ala* (no. 5659), *Tashfeetul-Muhadditheen* (1/191), *Musnad Ahmad* (2/44 and 84), *al-Kaamil* of Ibn Adiyy (2/455 and 5/1998) and other sources.

9. From a footnote of Ahmad Shaakir to the *Musnad* (no. 4835).

which the *Ummah* is suffering has produced a very grave effect which will ruin its people if they do not arouse from their slumber and awaken from their sleep - and this humiliation is disagreement and divergence.

Hadeeth Three
Disagreement and Divergence

From 'Abdullaah ibn Mas'ood (*radiyallaahu 'anhuma*) who said:

خَطَّ لَنَا رسولُ اللهِ ﷺ خَطًّا ثم قال: « هَذا سَبِيلُ اللهِ » ، ثم خَطَّ
خُطوطاً عن يَمِينِهِ وَعَنْ شِمالِهِ، ثم قال:
« هَذِه سُبُلٌ مُتَفَرِّقَةٌ، على كُلِّ سَبِيلٍ منها شَيْطَانٌ يَدعو إليه » .

Allaah's Messenger (ﷺ) drew a line for us, then he said, "This is Allaah's Way." Then he drew lines to its' right and its' left, and said, "These are different ways, upon each of these ways is a devil calling to it." Then he recited:

وَأَنَّ هَٰذَا صِرَٰطِى مُسْتَقِيمًا فَٱتَّبِعُوهُ وَلَا تَتَّبِعُواْ ٱلسُّبُلَ
فَتَفَرَّقَ بِكُمْ عَن سَبِيلِهِۦ

"And verily this is my Straight Path, so follow it, and do not follow (other) paths for they will separate you away from His Path."[10,11]

This *hadeeth* makes clear a very important matter which should be considered and reflected upon - and it is the disagreement within the *Ummah* concerning the Straight Prophetic Path, which has led to the splitting of the *Ummah*.

---

10. Soorah al-An'aam (6):153

11. Reported by at-Tayaalisee (no. 244) and from him Ahmad (1/435, 465) with a chain of narration that is of the level of *hasan* as it contains 'Aasim ibn Bahdalah about whom there is some slight talk, and we have spoken about this *hadeeth* in our checking of the book *al-Junnah Fee Takhreejis Sunnah* (no. 5-6) of Ibn Nasr al-Marwazee.

Hadeeth Four
The Splitting of the Ummah

From Anas ibn Maalik (*radiyallaahu 'anhu*) **who said that Allaah's Messenger (ﷺ) said,**

« تَفْتَرِقُ هذه الأُمَّةُ على ثلاثٍ وسبعينَ فِرقةً، كلُّهم في النَّارِ إلاَّ واحِدَةً » قالوا: وما هي تِلْكَ الفِرْقَةُ؟ قال:
« ما أنا عَلَيْهِ اليَوْمَ وَأَصْحَابِي ».

"This *Ummah* will split into seventy-three sects, all of them in the Fire (of Hell) except one." They asked, "And what is that sect?" He said, "That which I and my Companions are upon today."[12]

The splitting indicated in this *hadeeth* is a reality which has occurred, even a blind person would not deny it, nor a proud person refuse to believe it. The *hadeeth* itself contains an indication of the way to resolve this problem of sectarian splitting and that is clinging to that which the Prophet (ﷺ) and his Companions were upon. But what is the way?

---

12. Reported by at-Tabaraanee in *al-Mu'jamus-Sagheer* (no. 724), Bahshal in *Taareekh Waasit* (p.196) and from him al-'Uqailee in *ad-Du'afaa* (2/262). The *hadeeth* has another chain of narration which supports it, it is reported by at-Tirmidhee (no. 2641) and al-Haakim (1/125). In summary the *hadeeth* is *hasan* due to its two chains.

Hadeeth Five
What is the Way?

From Hudhaifah ibn al-Yamaan (*radiyallaahu 'anhu*) **who said:**

كانَ النَّاسُ يَسْأَلُونَ رَسُولَ اللهِ ﷺ عن الخَيرِ، وكنتُ أَسْأَلُهُ عَنِ الشَّرِّ مَخَافَةَ أَنْ يُدرِكَنِي، فَقُلْتُ: يا رَسُولَ اللهِ، إِنَّا كُنَّا في جَاهِلِيّةٍ وشَرٍّ، فجاءَنا اللهُ بهٰذا الخَيْرِ، فهل بعدَ هذا الخَيرِ مِن شرٍّ؟ قال: «نعم» قلتُ: وهل بعد ذلك الشَّرِّ من خيرٍ؟ قال: «نعم، وفيه دَخَنٌ» قلتُ: وما دَخَنُهُ؟ قال:

«قَوْمٌ يَهْدُونَ بِغَيرِ هَدِيِي، تَعْرِفُ منهُم وَتُنْكِرُ».

قُلْتُ: فهل بعد ذلك الخَيرِ مِن شرٍّ؟ قال:

«نعم، دَعاةٌ على أبوابِ جَهَنَّمَ، مَن أجابَهُم إليها! قَذَفُوهُ فيها».

قُلْتُ: يا رسولَ اللهِ! صِفْهُم لنا، قال:

«هُمْ مِن جِلْدَتِنَا وَيَتَكَلَّمُونَ بِأَلْسِنَتِنَا».

قُلتُ: فما تَأْمُرُنِي إِنْ أَدرَكَنِي ذلك؟ قال:

«تَلْزَمُ جماعَةَ المُسْلِمِينَ وإمَامَهُم».

قُلتُ: فإِن لم تَكُنْ لهم جَمَاعَةٌ ولا إمامٌ؟ قال:

«فاعْتَزِل تِلْكَ الفِرَقَ كُلَّها، ولو أَنْ تَعَضَّ بِأَصْلِ شَجَرةٍ حتى يُدرِكَكَ المَوْتُ وأنتَ على ذلك».

The people used to ask Allaah's Messenger (ﷺ) about the good, and I used to ask about the evil out of fear that it would reach me. So I asked, "O Messenger of Allaah (ﷺ) we were living in ignorance and evil, then Allaah brought this good to us. So will there be any evil

15

after this good?" He replied, "Yes." I then asked, "Will there be any good after that evil?" He replied, "Yes, but it will be tainted." So I asked, "What will be its taint?" He replied, "A people who guide others to other than my way, you will approve of some of their deeds and disapprove of others." I further enquired, "Then is there any evil after that good?" He said, "Yes, callers at the gates of Hell - whoever responds to their call, they will throw him into the Fire." I then said, "O Messenger of Allaah describe them to us." He said, "They will be from our people and speak our language." I asked, "So what do you order me to do if that reaches me?" He said, "Stick to the united body (jamaa'ah) of the Muslims and their Ruler (imaam)." I further asked, "What if they have neither a united body nor a Ruler?" He replied, "Then keep away from all of those sects, even if you have to bite upon the roots of a tree until death reaches you while you are in that state."[13]

This hadeeth shows the general principles which the Muslim should follow. The most important matter here is avoidance of those things which put the Muslim to trial in his everyday life and in his Deen; particularly when the united body (jamaa'ah) of the Muslims is not to be found, under the leadership of the single imaam who establishes the Islamic laws and punishments.

This was indicated by Imaam at-Tabaree[14] who said, "The hadeeth shows that when the people do not have a (single) imaam, and the people are divided into separate groups, then no one is to be followed in that state of

---

13. Reported al-Bukhaaree (eng. trans. vol. 9 p. 159-160) and Muslim (eng. trans. vol. 3, p.1028, no. 4553).

14. Al-Haafidh Ibn Hajr reports it from him in Fathhul-Baaree (13/37).

discord[15] and he should keep away from all of them if he is able to - for fear that he may fall into evil."

This is the correct way today when Islaam is a stranger and the carriers of the *Deen* and the callers to it are being lost. But the correct way needs to be clarified.

---

15. This does not mean that *da'wah* should come to a halt, or that ordering good and forbidding evil should cease as will be shown later.

17

Hadeeth Six
Clarification of the Way

From al-'Irbaad ibn Saariyah (*radiyallaahu 'anhu*) who said:

وَعَظَنَا رَسُولُ اللهِ ﷺ مَوْعِظَةً ذَرَفَتْ منها العُيُونُ، وَوَجِلَتْ منها
القُلُوبُ، فَقُلْنَا: يا رَسُولَ اللهِ، إنَّ هٰذه لَمَوْعِظَةُ مُوَدِّعٍ فَماذا تَعْهَدُ
إِلَيْنَا؟ قال:

« قد تركتُكم على البَيْضَاءِ، لَيْلِها كَنَهَارِها، لا يزيغُ عنها بَعْدِي إلاَّ
هَالِكٌ، وَمَن يَعِشْ منكم فَسَيَرى اختِلافاً كَثِيراً، فَعَلَيْكُمْ بِما عَرَفْتُم مِن
سُنَّتِي، وَسُنَّةِ الخُلَفَاءِ الرَّاشدين المَهْدِيِّينَ، عَضُّوا عَلَيْهَا بِالنَّوَاجِذِ، وعليكم
بِالطَّاعةِ، وإن عَبْداً حَبَشِيّاً، فَإنَّمَا المُؤْمِنُ كالجَمَلِ الأَنِفِ، حَيْثُمَا قِيدَ
انْقَادَ. »

Allaah's Messenger (ﷺ) gave us an admonition which caused the eyes to shed tears and the hearts to fear, so we said, "O Messenger of Allaah, this is as if it were a farewell sermon, so with what do you counsel us?" So he said, "I have left you upon clear proof, its night is like its day, no one deviates from it except one who is destroyed, and whoever lives (long) from amongst you will see great controversy. So stick to what you know from my *Sunnah* and the *Sunnah* of the orthodox, rightly-guided caliphs - cling to that with your molar teeth, and stick to obedience even if it is to an Abyssinian slave, since the believer is like the submissive camel, wherever he is led, he follows."[16]

---

16. Reported by Ahmad (4/126), Ibn Maajah (no. 43), al-Haakim (1/96), al-Baihaqee in *al-Madkhal* (no. 51) and Aboo 'Ubayd in *al-Khutub Wal-Mawaa'iz* (no. 20) by way of 'Abdur-Rahmaan ibn 'Amr as-Sulamee from him. Its chain of narration is *hasan*.

So the way is white and pure, manifest and untainted, such that its night is just like its day! Despite this, people stumble around blindly, not knowing the truth, nor avoiding that which is false - so what is the reason for this?

Is it because the way is hidden? No, the way is known but its signposts are still unclear to many people. Therefore we must know what are the signposts of the way.

Hadeeth Seven
Signposts of the Way

From Ibn 'Abbaas (*radiyallaahu 'anhuma*) who said that Allaah's Messenger (ﷺ) addressed the people in the Farewell Hajj and said:

« يَا أَيُّهَا النَّاسُ! إِنِّي قد تَرَكْتُ فِيكم ما إِنِ اغْتَصَمْتُمْ بِهِ فَلَنْ تَضِلُّوا أَبَدَا: كِتَابَ اللهِ وَسُنَّتِي ».

O people, I have left amongst you that which if you cling onto you will never go astray: The Book of Allaah and my *Sunnah*.[17]

So the two main signposts for this way are the Book and the *Sunnah*, and there is no escape from the obligation of accepting them and referring to them, keeping far away from the opinions of the people of vain desires and those who seek to judge by personal experience and their own feelings.

Perhaps the question will occur to some people: Does anybody deny these two points of reference? And the answer is: Yes, but their denial is hidden and not apparent since no one, no matter how deeply he is drowned in misguidance, will have the nerve to deny them openly!

But there is a fine point here which must be noted and mentioned, that being the matter of how these two reference points are to be understood - and that it can only be by the criterion...

---

17. Reported by al-Haakim (1/93), al-Baihaqee (10/114) and Ibn Hazm in *al-Ahkaam* (6/108) by way of Tawr ibn Zayd ad-Deelee from Ikrimah, from him. This chain of narration is *hasan*.

Hadeeth Eight
The Criterion

From Aboo Hurairah (*radiyallaahu 'anhu*) who said:

سُئِلَ رسُولُ اللهِ ﷺ: أيُّ النَّاسِ خَيْرٌ؟ فقال:
«أنا، والذين مَعِي، ثم الَّذين على الأثر، ثم الَّذين على الأثر» ثم
كأنَّهُ رفَضَ مَن بَقِيَ.

Allaah's Messenger (ﷺ) was asked, "Which of the people are the best?" So he replied, "Myself and those with me, then those who follow them, then those who follow them." Then it is as if he declined those who remained.[18]

The criterion for the correct understanding of the Book and the *Sunnah* is the practice of the Companions, and those who followed their way after them, then those who came after them, following in their footsteps, since they are the best of the people. Whereas other than them were declined and those not following their way contain no good.

So whoever claims to be following the Book and the *Sunnah* without this criterion, then without a doubt he is fooling himself.

Even though very few of the Muslims follow this rightly-guided methodology (*manhaj*), it is certain that good will remain (present).

---

18. Reported by Ahmad (2/297, 340) and Aboo Nu'aim in *al-Imaamah* (no. 3) by way of Muhammad ibn 'Ajlaan, from his father, from him. This chain of narration is of the level of *hasan* due to what is said concerning Ibn 'Ajlaan. The basis of this *hadeeth* is found in *Saheeh Muslim* and *Saheeh al-Bukhaaree* from a number of the Companions; I have quoted this wording due to its singularity - along with its chain of narration which is *hasan*.

Hadeeth Nine
Good will Remain

From Mu'aawiyah *(radiyallaahu 'anhu)*, who said that Allaah's Messenger (ﷺ) said:

» لاَ تَزَالُ طَائِفَةٌ مِن أُمَّتِي قَائِمَةٌ بِأَمْرِ اللهِ، لا يضرُّهُم مَن خَذَلَهُم، ولا مَن خَالَفَهُم، حَتَّى يَأْتِيَ أَمْرُ اللهِ، وَهُمْ ظَاهِرُونَ على النَّاسِ. «

There will not cease to be a group of my *Ummah*, obedient to Allaah's orders. They will not be harmed by those who desert them, nor those who oppose them until Allaah's order comes about and they have ascendancy over the people.[19]

So this good will remain throughout the ages and in all the lands and will not be eliminated by evil plots, nor subdued by the plans of the deceitful. So whoever deserts them - from the offspring of this group, those whom the devils of desires and doubts have led astray - then it will not harm this group, and neither will those who openly oppose it and show enmity to it. Rather it is established by the order of Allaah, awaiting the order of Allaah. And regarding every individual from this group - then the basis of his call is self-correction and rectification of others.

---

19. Reported by al-Bukhaaree (eng. trans. vol. 9, p.414, no. 4719) and Muslim (eng. trans. vol. 3, p.1061, no. 4719).

Hadeeth Ten
Rectification of Oneself and Others

From Sahl ibn S'ad *(radiyallaahu 'anhu)* **who said that Allaah's Messenger (ﷺ) said:**

« إنَّ الإسلامَ بدأ غريباً وسيعود غريباً، فطُوبى للغُرباء » .

قالوا: يا رسولَ اللهِ! وما الغُرباء؟ قال:

« الَّذِينَ يُصلحون عند فَسَادِ النَّاسِ » .

Islaam began as a stranger and will return to being a stranger, so *tooba* (a certain huge tree in Paradise) is for *the strangers (al-Ghurabaa)*. They asked, "O Messenger of Allaah! Who are the strangers?" He replied, "Those who rectify [themselves and others][20] when the people are corrupt."[21]

So the fact that Islaam is a stranger amongst the people is something which increases a believer's *eemaan*, and raises his level of certainty, and strengthens his resolve, since he is righteous himself and seeks to rectify others. He is not alone in being a stranger, indeed in this regard he is like many of the Prophets *('alayhimus salaam)*, as the Prophet (ﷺ) said,

---

20. The Arabic word read with a *dammah: yuslihoon* means to correct others, and read with a *fathha: yaslihoon* means self-correction.

21. Reported by at-Tabaraanee in *al-Kabeer* (no. 5867) and in *as-Sagheer* (no. 290), al-Qudaa'ee (no. 1055) and ad-Doolaabee (1/193) by way of Bakr ibn Sulaim as-Sawwaaf from Aboo Haazim from him - and its chain of narration is *saheeh*. The *hadeeth* has other chains of narration from a number of the Companions.

"The nations were presented before me, and I saw a prophet with whom there was a small group, and a prophet with whom there was a single man or two men, and a prophet with nobody with him..." [22]

"And this contains a clear proof that the number of followers, whether large or small, is not a means of knowing whether the caller is upon the truth or falsehood." [23]

A persons' correction of himself and others is built upon three principles, the first of which is: *Tawheed* of Allaah - making all of ones' worship for Allaah alone.

22. Reported by al-Bukhaaree (eng. trans. vol. 7, p.434, no. 648) and Muslim (eng. trans. vol. 1, p.141, no. 625).

23. Shaikh al-Albaanee in *as-Silsilatus-Saheehah* (1/684).

Hadeeth Eleven
Making all Worship for Allaah Alone (*Tawheed*)

From Ibn 'Abbaas *(radiyallaahu 'anhuma)* who said: When the Prophet (ﷺ) sent Mu'aadh *(radiyallaahu 'anhu)* to the people of Yemen he said to him:

« إِنَّكَ تَقْدِمُ عَلَى قَوْمٍ مِنْ أَهْلِ الكتابِ، فَلْيَكُنْ أَوَّلَ مَا تَدعوهم إلى : أَنْ يُوَحِّدُوا اللهَ تعالى، فإذا عَرَفُوا ذلك: فَأَخْبِرْهُمْ أَنَّ اللهَ فَرَضَ عليهم خَمْسَ صَلَواتٍ في يومِهِمْ وَلَيْلَتِهِم، فَإِذا صَلَّوْا: فَأَخْبِرْهُمْ أَنَّ اللهَ افْتَرَضَ عليهم زكاةَ أموالِهم تُؤْخَذُ مِن غَنِيِّهِمْ فَتُرَدُّ على فقيرِهِمْ، فإذا أَقَرُّوا بذلك فَخُذْ منهم، وَتَوَقَّ كَرائِمَ أَموالِ النَّاسِ. »

You are going to a nation from the people of the Book, so let the first thing that you call them to be that they should make all worship solely for Allaah, the Most High. So if they realize that, then inform them that Allaah has obligated upon them five prayers in the day and night. If they pray then inform them that Allaah has obligated upon them *zakaat* from their wealth - to be taken from their rich and given to their poor. If they accept that then take it from them, but avoid the best part of the people's property.[24]

This is the first matter which it is obligatory for a person to know since without it a person does not enter Islaam. So singling out Allaah, the One free from all imperfections, for all worship (*Tawheed*), is the first half of the declaration of *Tawheed*: *Laa ilaaha illallaah* i.e. None has the right to be

---

24. Reported by al-Bukhaaree (eng. trans. vol. 9, p. 348, no. 469) and Muslim (eng. trans. vol. 1, p. 15, no. 28).

worshipped but Allaah, the One free of all imperfections and the Most High. The other half of this pure and noble saying is: *Muhammadun Rasoolullaah* which means: None has the right to be followed (unquestioningly) except Allaah's Messenger (ﷺ) and this is the second foundation: *al-Ittibaa'* (following Allaah's Messenger (ﷺ)).

Hadeeth Twelve
Following Allaah's Messenger (ﷺ) (Al-Ittibaa')

From Jaabir ibn 'Abdullaah (radiyallaahu 'anhu) who said:

كان رسولُ اللهِ ﷺ إذا خَطَبَ احْمَرَّت عَيْناه، وعَلاَ صَوْتُهُ، واشْتَدَّ
غَضَبُهُ، حتى كأنَّه مُنذِرُ جَيْشٍ، يقولُ: صَبَّحكم ومَسَّاكم، ويقول:
«بُعِثْتُ أَنا والساعَةُ كهاتَين» ويَقْرِنُ بين إصْبَعَيْهِ السَّبابةِ
والوُسْطىٰ، ويقولُ:
«أمَّا بَعْدُ، فإنَّ خيرَ الحديثِ كتابُ اللهِ، وخَيْرَ الهُدىٰ هُدىٰ مُحَمَّد
وشَرَّ الأمورِ مُحْدثاتُها، وكُلَّ بِدعةٍ ضَلالَةٌ.»

When Allaah's Messenger (ﷺ) gave a *khutbah* (sermon) his eyes became reddened, his voice raised, and his anger grew to the extent that it were as if he were one exhorting an army saying, "They will attack you morning and evening," and he would say, "I have been sent along with the (Last) Hour like these two" and he joined his forefinger and middle finger, and would say, "To proceed: Indeed the best speech is the book of Allaah and the best guidance is the guidance of Muhammad (ﷺ), and the worst of affairs are the newly invented matters, and every innovation is misguidance."[25]

This is also stated by the scholars of *tafseer* in explanation of the saying of Allaah, the Most High:

---

25. Reported by Muslim (eng. trans. vol.2, p. 410, no. 1885) and others. Some of those who report the *hadeeth* report the addition *"And all misguidance is in the Fire."* And it's chain of narration is *saheeh* as I have explained in my footnotes to *Juz-uttibaa-is-Sunan Wajtinaabil-Bida* (no. 1) of ad-Diyaa-al-Maqdisee.

$$بَلَىٰ مَنْ أَسْلَمَ وَجْهَهُۥ لِلَّهِ وَهُوَ مُحْسِنٌ فَلَهُۥٓ أَجْرُهُۥ عِندَ رَبِّهِۦ وَلَا خَوْفٌ عَلَيْهِمْ وَلَا هُمْ يَحْزَنُونَ ۝$$

"Yes, but whoever submits his face (himself) to Allaah and he is a *muhsin* then his reward is with his Lord, on such shall there be no fear, nor shall they grieve." [26]

They say *muhsin* means: He follows the Messenger (ﷺ) in it, since there are two conditions for the acceptability of an action: Firstly, that it is purely for Allaah alone and secondly that it is correct, i.e. conforming to the *Sharee'ah*. So, if it is done purely (for Allaah), but is not a correct action then it will not be accepted. [27]

So if the reality of the two principles we have mentioned settles in the heart of the servant, i.e. *Tawheed* and *Ittibaa'*, then that will be the key to the third principle from the principles of calling to Islaam, which is *Tazkiyah* (purification).

---

26. Soorah al-Baqarah(2):112

27. *Tafseer Ibn Katheer* (1/231).

Hadeeth Thirteen
Tazkiyah (Purification)

From Aboo Hurairah *(radiyallaahu 'anhu)* who said:

قال رسول الله ﷺ : « مَن يأخذ عَنِّي هؤلاءِ الكلماتِ فيعْمَلَ بِهِنَّ ،
أو يُعَلِّمَ مَن يعملُ بِهِنَّ؟ »، فقال أبو هُرَيرَة: فَقُلْتُ: أنا يا رسولَ الله ،
فأخذَ بِيَدي، فَعَدَّ خَمْساً، قال:

« اتَّقِ المحارِمَ تَكُنْ أعبَدَ الناسِ ، وارضَ بما قَسَمَ اللهُ لك تَكُنْ
أغنى النَّاسِ ، وأحسِنْ إلى جارِكَ تَكُنْ مُؤْمِناً، وَأحِبَّ للنَّاسِ ما
تُحِبُّ لِنَفْسِكَ تَكُنْ مُسْلِماً، ولا تُكْثِرِ الضَّحِكَ، فإنَّ كَثْرَةَ الضَّحِكِ تُمِيتُ
القَلْبَ » .

Allaah's Messenger (ﷺ) said, "Who will take these words from me and act upon them, or teach those who will act upon them?" So I said, "I (will) O Messenger of Allaah." So he took hold of my hand and counted out five, saying, "Keep away from the forbidden things - you will be the most devout of the people; be pleased with what Allaah has given you - you will be the richest of people; treat your neighbour well - you will be a Believer; love for the people (the good) which you love for yourself - you will be a Muslim; and do not laugh greatly for too much laughter kills off the heart."[28]

---

28. Reported by at-Tirmidhee (no. 2306), Ahmad (2/310), al-Kharaaitee in *Makaarimul-Akhlaaq* (p. 42), Aboo Ya'laa (no. 6240) and Aboo Ahmad al-Haakim in *al-Kunaa* (q. 2572) it is also reported through another chain of narration - It is reported by Ibn Maajah (no. 4217), Aboo Nu'aim in *al-Hulyah* (10/365) and in *Dhikr Akhbaar Isbahaan* (2/302), Aboo Ya'laa (no. 5865) and al-Baihaqee in *az-Zuhd* (no. 818) by way of Aboo Rajaa, from Burd ibn Sinaan, from Makhool, from Waatilah, from Aboo Hurairah. The *hadeeth* is *hasan* if Allaah wills.

Purification (tazkiyah) is freeing the soul from that which pollutes it and from diseases with which Shaitaan tries to assault the righteous servants of Allaah who worship Him alone. So whenever a person purifies himself he draws closer to his Lord and humbles to the orders of His Creator, and those things which are very hard for ailing souls become easy for him. Concerning this Allaah, the Most High says:

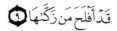

"Indeed he succeeds who purifies his ownself."[29]

The caller (daa'ee) whilst putting the three principles of da'wah into practice must never forget the nature of the Deen.

---

29. Soorah ash-Shams (91):9.

Hadeeth Fourteen
The Nature of the *Deen*

From Aboo Moosa al-Ash'aree (*radiyallaahu 'anhu*) who said:

كانَ رسولُ اللهِ ﷺ إذا بَعَثَ أحداً مِن أصحابِهِ في بَعْضِ أمرِه
قال :

« بَشِّروا ولا تُنَفِّروا، وَيَسِّروا ولا تُعَسِّروا » .

When Allaah's Messenger (ﷺ) sent one of his Companions on a mission he would say, "Give good tidings and do not cause (people) to flee; make things easy and do not make things difficult."[30]

So it (the *Deen*) is built upon giving good tidings not upon causing the people to run away; upon making things easy and not making them difficult. If one gives admonition to anyone then it must be given with softness and wisdom. If one orders good then it must be done with mildness and causing ease. If one forbids evil then it must be done with mercy and compassion. With these attributes, together with what has preceded, we will move forward with our *Deen* on the way to being foremost in affairs but without these attributes we can only await the appearance of defects.

---

30. Reported by Muslim (eng. trans. vol. 3, p. 944, no. 4297).

Hadeeth Fifteen
The Appearance of Defects

From Aboo Hurairah *(radiyallaahu 'anhu)* **who said:**

بينما النبيُّ ﷺ في مجلسٍ يُحَدِّثُ القومَ جاءه أعرابيٌّ، فقال: متى
الساعةُ؟ فمضى رسولُ اللهِ ﷺ يُحَدِّثُ، فقال بعضُ القومِ: سَمِعَ ما قالَ
فَكَرِهَ ما قالَ، وقال بعضُهم: بل لم يسمعْ، حتى إذا قضى حديثَه قال:
«أينَ أُراهُ السائلُ عن الساعةِ»؟ قال: ها أنا يا رسولَ اللهِ، قال:
«فإذا ضُيِّعَتِ الأمانةُ فانتظِرِ الساعةَ»، قال: كيفَ إضاعتُها؟ قال:
«إذا وُسِّدَ الأمرُ إلى غَيرِ أهلِهِ فانْتَظِرِ الساعةَ».

**Whilst Allaah's Messenger (ﷺ) was speaking to the
people in a gathering a bedouin came to him and asked,
"When is the Last Hour?" So Allaah's Messenger (ﷺ)
continued speaking. Some of the people said, "He heard
what he said but did not like it," while others said,
"Rather he did not hear." When he finished his speech
he said, "Where is the questioner who asked about the
Hour?" He said, "Here I am O Messenger of Allaah."
He said, "When honesty is lost then await the Hour."
He asked, "How will it be lost?" He said, "When
authority is given to unfit persons then await the
Hour."[31]**

If a person over estimates his own status and his heart reaches out for
leadership which he is not ready for then that will be the beginning of the
end for him. In this regard it is said: *Whoever assumes leadership before his
time, has invited his own humiliation!* So if this is the case then we must be
aware of the cause of the defects.

---

31. Reported by al-Bukhaaree in his *Saheeh* (eng. trans. vol. 1, p. 50, no. 56).

Hadeeth Sixteen
The Cause of the Defects

From 'Abdullaah ibn 'Umar (*radiyallaahu 'anhumaa*) who said: I heard Allaah's Messenger (ﷺ) say:

« إِنَّمَا النَّاسُ كالإِبِلِ المِئَةِ، لا تَكادُ تَجِدُ فيها راحِلَةً » .

Indeed people are like camels, out of a hundred you will hardly find a single one suitable to ride.[32]

"The *hadeeth* comprises of a truthful statement of fact and beneficial guidance. As regards the statement of fact then he (ﷺ) informed us that deficiency is something found in most of the people and that completeness, or nearness to it, is rare amongst them. Just like a hundred camels, which seems like a large number, but if you need one for carrying or riding, or coming and going you will hardly be able to find one. The majority of people are the same: if you were to select from them one who is suitable for teaching, giving religious verdicts (*fataawa*) or leadership then you would hardly find anyone to carry out the task properly. This is the state of affairs, because man is unjust and ignorant, and injustice and ignorance are the cause of defects which prevent the attainment of perfection or completeness. As regards the guidance, then this narration contains an indication from him (ﷺ) that the whole *Ummah* should hasten together and strive hard to prepare men who are suitable for taking charge of matters of importance and the running of public affairs, beneficial to the people as a whole."[33]

---

32. Reported by al-Bukhaaree (eng. trans. vol. 8, p. 334, no. 505) and Muslim (eng. trans. vol. 4, p. 1353, no. 6179).

33. *Bahjatul-Abraar* (p.316) of the great scholar 'Abdur Rahman As-Sa'dee.

Hadeeth Seventeen
How to Rectify the Defects

From Tameem ad-Daaree (*radiyallaahu 'anhu*) who said that Allaah's Messenger (ﷺ) said:

« الدِّينُ النَّصِيحَةُ، الدِّينُ النَّصِيحَةُ، الدِّينُ النَّصِيحَةُ » .

قُلْنَا: لِمَنْ يا رسولَ اللهِ؟ قال:

« لِلَّهِ، ولكتابِهِ، ولرسولِه، وَلأَئِمَّةِ الْمُسْلِمِينَ وعامَّتِهمْ » .

"The *Deen* is sincerity.[34] The *Deen* is sincerity. The *Deen* is sincerity." We asked, "To whom O Messenger of Allaah?" He replied, "To Allaah, to His Book, to His Messenger, to the leaders of the Muslims and their common folk."[35]

Through sincerity and sincere advising alone can we correct and reform ourselves and rectify our defects. It is therefore an obligation which must not be abandoned, as it will lead to further good which will not be abandoned except by one who has lost his mind and who leaves his portion of good. [36]

The faithful and sincere adviser has a distinguishing sign: when he wishes to enhance the one he is advising he advises him privately, whereas the sign of the one who wishes to disgrace him is that he advises him in public.[37]

---

34. Arabic: *Naseehah*: This is a comprehensive word of vast meaning which includes having sincerity towards each other, wishing everything good for one another and giving honest and sincere advice as is fully explained in *Sharh Saheeh Muslim* of an-Nawawee (2/37-39) [Translator's note]

35. Reported by Muslim (no. 55) [eng. trans. vol.1, p.37, no. 98].

36. *Ar-Risaalah* (no. 170) of Imaam ash-Shaafi'ee.

37. *Rawtadul-Uqalaa* (p. 196) of Ibn Hibbaan.

So through sincerity and sincere advising we will, if Allaah wills, reach the state of affairs which we desire.

Hadeeth Eighteen
The State of Affairs which we Desire

From Aboo Hurairah *(radiyallaahu 'anhu)* who said that Allaah's Messenger (ﷺ) said:

« إِنَّ مِنْ عِبَادِ اللهِ عِبَادًا لَيْسُوا بِأَنْبِيَاءَ ، يَغْبِطُهُمُ الْأَنْبِيَاءُ وَالشُّهَدَاءُ »
قِيلَ : مَنْ هُمْ؟ لَعَلَّنَا نُحِبُّهُمْ! قَالَ :
« هُمْ قَوْمٌ تَحَابُّوا بِنُورِ اللهِ مِنْ غَيْرِ أَرْحَامٍ وَلَا أَنْسَابٍ ، وُجُوهُهُمْ نُورٌ ،
عَلَى مَنَابِرَ مِنْ نُورٍ ، لَا يَخَافُونَ إِذَا خَافَ النَّاسُ ، وَلَا يَحْزَنُونَ إِذَا حَزِنَ
النَّاسُ » .

Indeed from amongst the servants of Allaah there are servants who are not Prophets whom the Prophets and Martyrs will envy.[38] It was asked, "Who are they? So that we may love them." He replied, "They are a people who love each other due to Allaah's light, not because of relationship or kinship, their faces being light, upon pulpits of light. They do not fear when the people fear, nor do they grieve when the people grieve." Then he recited:

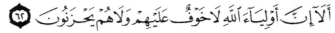

"No doubt! Verily, the friends of Allaah, no fear shall come upon them nor shall they grieve."[39,40]

---

38. Arabic: *Ghabt*: Where one wishes to achieve the good seen with another person - but does not wish it to cease for that other person [Translator's note].

39. Reported by at-Tabaree in his *Tafseer* (11/132) and Ibn Hibbaan in his *Saheeh* (no. 2508 in *az-Zawaa'id*). It's chain of narration is *hasan*.

40. Soorah Yoonus (10):62.

Through loving for the sake of Allaah, the One free of all imperfections, the callers will attain everything good, and through it their hearts will become united and their spirits raised high. This loving is made obligatory upon them by the great and pure *Deen* of Islaam not by restrictive partisanship or detestable party-spirit! This mutual love obligates the Muslims and the callers to fulfil those things which are a right upon them.

Hadeeth Nineteen
The Rights (of a Muslim)

From Aboo Hurairah *(radiyallaahu 'anhu)* **who said that Allaah's Messenger (ﷺ) said:**

« حَقُّ المُسْلِمِ على المُسْلِمِ سِتٌّ . »

قالوا: ماهُنَّ يا رسولَ اللهِ؟ قال:

« إذا لَقِيَه سَلَّمَ عليهِ، وإذا دَعاهُ أَجابه، وإذا اسْتَنْصَحَ نَصَحَهُ.
وإذا عَطَسَ فحَمِدَ اللهَ يُشَمِّتُهُ، وإذا مَرِضَ عَادَهُ، وإذا مات صَحِبهُ . »

The rights of a Muslim upon another Muslim are six. They asked, "What are they O Messenger of Allaah ?" He said, "When he meets him he greets him with *salaam*, when he invites him he responds, when he asks for his sincere advice he sincerely advises him, when he sneezes and praises Allaah he asks for Allaah's mercy for him, when he is ill he visits him, and when he dies he accompanies him (i.e. his funeral)."[41]

It is obligatory upon the caller that he fulfils these and other rights which his brothers and companions have upon him since they are a protective wall shielding *da'wah* from breaking apart, and protecting the caller from negligence. Thus they are a safeguard for himself and a protection for his brothers.

After what has preceded there are some comprehensive matters which every Muslim must be aware of and not forget, and from them is: The caller's beginning.

---

41. Reported by Muslim (no. 2162) [eng. trans. vol.3, p.1183, no. 5379].

Hadeeth Twenty
The Caller's Beginning

From Ibn 'Umar (*radiyallaahu 'anhuma*) who said that Allaah's Messenger (ﷺ) said:

« لِكُلِّ عَمَلٍ شِرَّةٌ ، وَلِكُلِّ شِرَّةٍ فَتْرَةٌ، فمن كانت فَتْرَتُهُ إلى سُنَّتي نقد اهْتدىٰ، ومن كانت فَتْرَتُهُ إلى غير ذلك فقد هلك » .

For every action there is a period of enthusiasm/activity, and for every period of enthusiasm/activity there is a period of rest/inactivity. So he whose period of rest/inactivity is in accordance with my *Sunnah* then he is rightly guided, but he whose period of rest accords with other than this, then he is destroyed.[42]

Every beginning is difficult, and the difficulty of beginning something will vary with different people. With regard to the Muslim who turns his face to calling to Allaah, the One free of all imperfections, then he will begin strongly since he wishes to practice all of the *Deen* and wishes to forbid every evil and so on...

However, after this initial enthusiasm and activity will come a period of inactivity and slackness, if he keeps to the Prophetic *Sunnah*, and still proceeds in the right direction then he has been guided aright and directed to what is correct.[43] But if not then he is destroyed and Allaah's refuge is sought. In this regard the way of the Pious Predecessors (*as-Salafus-Saalih*) was to point out

---

42. Reported by Ahmad (2/188 and 210) and others with a *saheeh isnaad*. Its sources are fully given in *Juz Ittibaa'is-Sunan* (no. 8) with my footnotes.

43. See *hadeeth* no. 34.

the people of the Sunnah (*Ahlus-Sunnah*). Ayyoob as-Sakhtiyaanee[44] said, "From the success of a youth or non-Arab is that Allaah guides him to a scholar of the *Sunnah*."[45]

Ibn Shawdhab[46] said, "From Allaah's blessings upon a youth when he turns to worship is that he is given a brother who is a follower of the *Sunnah* encouraging him upon it."[47]

So how surprising is the case of those who warn the Muslim youth against the scholars of the *Sunnah* and those who call to it by slandering them, belittling them, and defaming them!

The caller must realise to begin with the importance of keeping good company.

---

44. Scholar and worshipper from the Taabi'een. He lived in Basrah and died in the year 131H [Translator's note].

45. Reported by al-Laalikaa'ee in *Sharh Usoolis-Sunnah* (no. 30) and Ibn ul-Jawzee (p.18) and it is *hasan*.

46. 'Abdullaah ibn Shawdhab: from the generation after the Taabi'een. Originally from Balkh and finally settled in Jerusalem. Died 156H. [Translator's note].

47. Reported by al-Laalikaa'ee in *Sharh Usoolis-Sunnah* (no. 31) and Ibnul-Jawzee (p.18) and it is *hasan* like the previous one.

Hadeeth Twenty One
The Importance of Keeping Good Company

From Aboo Moosaa al-Asha'ree (*radiyallaahu 'anhu*) who said that Allaah's Messenger (ﷺ) said:

» مَثَلُ الجَلِيسِ الصَّالِحِ والجَلِيسِ السُّوءِ: كحامِلِ المِسْكِ.وَنَافِخِ الكِيرِ، فَحامِلُ المِسْكِ: إما أَنْ يُحْذِيَكَ وإِمَّا أَنْ تَبْتَاعَ مِنه، وَإِمَّا أَنْ تَجِدَ منه رِيحاً طَيِّبَةً. ونافِخُ الكِيرِ: إِمَّا أَنْ يَحْرِقَ ثِيَابَكَ، وإِمَّا أَنْ تَجِدَ مِنْهُ رِيحاً خَبِيثَةً. «

The example of a good companion and a bad companion is like that of the seller of musk, and the one who blows the blacksmith's bellows. So as for the seller of musk then either he will grant you some, or you buy some from him, or at least you enjoy a pleasant smell from him. As for the one who blows the blacksmith's bellows then either he will burn your clothes or you will get an offensive smell from him. [48]

So this is a completion of the previous chapter, through the like of this good company, Allaah saves those who are astray and guides the wicked. The scholars report[49] from Yoosuf ibn Asbaat[50] that he said, "My father was a

---

48. Reported by al-Bukhaaree (4/323) [eng. trans. vol.3, p.179, no. 314] and Muslim (no.2628) [eng. trans. vol.4, p.1383, no. 6361] .

49. *Sharh Usoolis-Sunnah* of al-Laalikaa'ee (no. 32).

50. A noble worshipper and student of Sufyaan ath-Thawree. He lived in Antioch and died in 195H. [Translator's note]

Qadaree,[51] and my maternal uncles were Raafidees[52] but Allaah saved me through Sufyaan."[53] And this is how it is, since "keeping company with the pious results in attainment of beneficial knowledge, noble manners and righteous actions, whereas keeping company with the wicked prevents all of that."[54]

So if the caller stays firm upon the true path, keeping good company, with the people of the *Sunnah*, then it is upon him to uphold the main pillar (mainstay) of *da'wah*.

---

51. A sect who deny Allaah's Predecree [Translator's note].

52. Extreme Shee'ah who revile the Companions. [Translator's note]

53. i.e. Sufyaan ath-Thawree, the Imaam of the *Sunnah*.

54. *Bahjatul-Abraar* (p.226) of Shaikh 'Abdur-Rahmaan as-Sa'dee.

Hadeeth Twenty Two
The Main Pillar of *Da'wah*

From Ibn Mas'ood *(radiyallaahu 'anhuma)* who said that Allaah's Messenger (ﷺ) said:

« ما مِنْ نَبِيٍّ بَعَثَهُ اللهُ فِي أُمَّةٍ قَبْلِي، إِلاَّ كَانَ لهُ مِنْ أُمَّتِهِ حَوَارِيُّونَ ، وأَصْحَابٌ ، يَأْخُذُونَ بِسُنَّتِهِ وَيَقْتَدُونَ بِأمرِه، ثُمَّ إِنَّها تَخْلُفُ مِن بعدِهم خُلُوفٌ ، يقولون ما لا يفعلون، ويفعلون ما لا يُؤمَرُون، فَمَنْ جَاهَدَهم بِيدِه فهو مُؤمِنٌ، وَمَن جَاهَدَهم بِلسانِه فهو مُؤمِنٌ، ومَن جَاهَدَهم بِقلبِه فهو مُؤمِنٌ، ليس وراءَ ذلك من الإيمانِ حَبَّةُ خَرْدَلٍ . »

There was not a prophet sent to a people before me except that he had helpers and companions who took hold of his *sunnah* and followed his orders, then after them came those who said that which they did not do, and did what they were not ordered. So whoever strives against them with his hand is a Believer; whoever strives against them with his tongue is a Believer; and whoever strives against them with his heart, is a Believer, and there is not beyond that a mustard seed of faith (*eemaan*).[55]

The essence of *da'wah* and its main pillar, and its core and marrow is ordering the good and forbidding the evil (*al-Amr bil-Ma'roof wan-Nahy 'Anil-Munkar*). So if that does not take place, then Allaah's wrath descends and punishment comes upon everyone, as the Prophet (ﷺ) said:

---

55. Reported by Muslim (no. 50) [eng. trans. vol.1, p.34, no. 81].

There are no people amongst whom sins are committed, and they are stronger than those who commit them yet they do not prevent that, except that Allaah sends His punishment upon them all.[56]

Ordering good and forbidding evil has different levels as occurs in the *hadeeth* of this chapter, so the caller should not proceed to one level at the expense of another, rather he should proceed according to his capacity and capability. The Muslim when ordering good and forbidding evil should not, in doing so, abandon the manners of the caller.

---

56. The *hadeeth* is *hasan*. I have quoted its sources and discussed it in my notes upon *Tashabbuhul-Khasees* (p.29) of al-Haafidh adh-Dhahabee.

(It is reported by Ahmad, Aboo Daawood, Ibn Maajah and Ibn Hibbaan. [Translator's note])

Hadeeth Twenty Three
Manners of the Caller

From Anas *(radiyallaahu 'anhu)* who said that Allaah's Messenger (ﷺ) said:

« ثلاثٌ مُهْلِكَاتٌ، وثلاثٌ مُنْجِيَاتٌ:

ثلاثٌ مُهْلِكَاتٌ، شُحٌّ مُطاعٌ، وهَوىً مُتَّبَعٌ، وإعجابُ المَرءِ بنفسِه .

وثلاثٌ مُنجياتٌ: خَشْيَةُ اللهِ في السِّرِّ والعلانية، والقَصْدُ في الفَقرِ والغِنى، والعَدْلُ في الغَضَبِ والرِّضا . »

Three things cause destruction and three things lead to salvation. The three things causing destruction are miserliness which is obeyed, desires which are followed and a person's self-admiration. The three things which lead to salvation are fear of Allaah in secret and in the open, moderation when rich or when poor, and being just when angry or when pleased.[57]

The manners indicated here are all the qualities of nobility and virtue - which are: the avoidance of every evil and performance of every good. From the evil manners which must be avoided are that a person admires himself! This is worsened if some ignorant people agree with him upon this and follow him - Allaah's refuge is sought - keeping in mind that this kind of following alone is something hated and repulsive to many of the wise scholars, since

---

57. Reported by al-Bazzaar (no. 81), al-'Uqaylee (3/447), Aboo Nu'aim (2/343) and al-Quda'ee (no. 325) by way of Ayyoob ibn 'Utbah, from al-Fadl ibn Bakr al-'Abdee, from Qataadah, from Anas.

The *hadeeth* has other chains of narration and in conclusion the *hadeeth* is of the level of *hasan* without a doubt due to its many chains. Therefore al-Mundharee said in *at-Targheeb wat-Tarheeb* (1/162): "It is reported by al-Bazzaar, al-Baihaqee and others and is reported from a group of the Companions, and its chains of narration even though none of them are free from criticism - yet together they are *hasan* if Allaah wills." I say: And that is what is correct.

'Aasim ibn Damrah[58] saw some people following a man, so he said, "It is a trial for the one who is followed and humiliation for the one following!"[59]

So how about one who admires himself and then attacks others in order to increase the number of his own followers! The like of him adds evil upon evil upon evil! So the noble manners of the caller spur him on to preserve or safeguard the protective wall of *da'wah*.

---

58. A *Taabi'ee* of Koofah who died in the year 174H. [Translator's note].

59. *Al-'Ilal* (2/16) of Ahmad ibn Hanbal.

Hadeeth Twenty Four
The Protective Wall of *Da'wah*

From Aboo Hurairah (*radiyallaahu 'anhu*) **who said that Allaah's Messenger** (ﷺ) **said:**

«لا يَفْرَكُ مُؤْمِنٌ مُؤْمِنَةً، إِنْ كَرِه مِنْهَا خُلُقا رَضِيَ منها آخَرَ» .

Let not a believing man hate a believing woman, if he dislikes one quality in her then he will be pleased with another.[60]

"This conduct which he (ﷺ) directed us to should be followed and applied with regard to all those whom we live and work with since its blessings with regard to both the *Deen* and the wordly affairs are many. A person behaving in this manner will give rest to his heart and will be led to maintain the obligatory and recommended rights others have over him, since completeness is something you will not find in the people, and it is sufficient excellence for a person that his faults are few enough to be counted. And contenting oneself with those things which you experience from people which are contrary to what you desire will make it easy for you to have good manners, to do what is good and to treat the people well."[61]

A further important benefit indicated by this noble *hadeeth* is:

"Removal of anxiety and unease, and that he remains cheerful and is constant in fulfilling the obligatory and recommended duties, and that he is at peace with others. But as for one who does not follow this guidance mentioned by the Prophet (ﷺ) rather he acts contrary to it and instead he notices peoples' faults and is blind to their virtues - then he will certainly live in a troubled

---

60. Reported by Muslim (no. 1469) [eng. trans. vol. 2, p.753, no. 3469].

61. *Bahajatul-Abraar* (p.175) of as-Sa'dee.

state, and any love he has for those whom he has relations with will certainly be affected by this, and many mutual rights which are obligatory will be abandoned."[62]

Whereas the caller being aware of the protective wall of *da'wah* will be a great help for him in truly perceiving the affairs.

---

62. *Al-Wassa'ilul-Mufeedah* (p.19) of as-Sa'dee with my footnotes.

Hadeeth Twenty Five
True Perception of Affairs

From 'Aa'ishah *(radiyallaahu 'anhaa)* who said that Allaah's Messenger (ﷺ) said:

«يا عائشةُ! لولا أنَّ قَوْمَكِ حَديثو عَهدٍ بجاهليةٍ، لأمرتُ بالبَيتِ نَهدِمَ، فَأدخَلْتُ فيه ما أُخرِج منه، وَأَلزَقْتُهُ بالأرضِ، وجعلتُ له بابَينِ: باباً شَرْقِياً، وباباً غَرْبِياً، فبلغتُ به أساسَ إبراهيمَ»...

O 'Aa'ishah! If it were not that your people had recently left ignorance I would have ordered that the House (Ka'bah) be dismantled, and I would have joined with it what was removed from it, and I would have levelled it with the ground, and I would have made two doors for it, one towards the east and one towards the west, so that I could build it upon the foundations laid by Ibraaheem.[63]

Through perception of the affairs everything will be given its due place, and the callers wisdom will be fully manifested so that he does not over-inflate a small matter, nor treat something serious as a minor matter, and he bears in mind the wisdom and rulings of the *Sharee'ah* in all his affairs.

However the people have gone beyond bounds in this matter, to the point that you see them giving no importance to the *Sunnah* and paying no attention to the truth! Striving, as they claim, to unite the *Ummah* and being careful not to hurt the peoples feelings! In my view this occurs from them as a

---

63. Reported by al-Bukhaaree (1/198) [eng. trans. vol.1, p.95, no. 128] and Muslim (no.1333) [eng. trans. vol.2, p.67, no. 3082].

reaction to that which some others do - whom you see causing a great furore over the slightest of matters!

The truth is between these two groups, so we do not remain silent about the truth and propagating the *Sunnah*, but at the same time we propagate it with full wisdom and in the best manner. Then if we see objections occurring or likely to occur we suffice with giving the reminder:

"...verily reminding profits the believers."[64]

And this is the way of the Prophet (ﷺ) in educating and cultivating (*Tarbiyah*).

---

64. Soorah adh-Dhaariyaat (51):55.

Hadeeth Twenty Six
The Way to Educate and Cultivate

From 'Aa'ishah *(radiyallaahu 'anhaa)* who said that Allaah's Messenger (ﷺ) said:

> « يا عائشةُ! إنَّ اللهَ رفيقٌ يُحِبُّ الرِّفْقَ، ويُعطي على الرِّفْقِ ما لا يُعطي على العُنفِ، وما لا يُعطي على ما سِواه . »

O 'Aa'ishah! Indeed Allaah is gentle and loves gentleness and gives due to gentleness, what he does not give due to harshness, and what he does not give due to other than it.[65]

The correct way to give *da'wah* is with gentleness and mildness, making things easy and avoiding harshness, severity and roughness. So in this way the people to whom we are giving *da'wah* will respond and will obtain Allaah's pleasure and pardon in the Hereafter! And from the comprehensive principles which should be known [as I indicated in explanation of *hadeeth* number nineteen] is the difference between knowledge and action upon it.

---

65. Reported by Muslim (no. 2593) [eng. trans. vol. 4, p.1370, no. 6273].

Hadeeth Twenty Seven
Between Having Knowledge and Action upon it

From Anas ibn Maalik *(radiyallaahu 'anhu)* **who said that Allaah's Messenger (ﷺ) said:**

« رَأَيْتُ لَيْلَةَ أُسْرِيَ بِي رِجَالاً تُقْرَضُ شِفَاهُهُم بِمَقَارِيضَ مِن نَارٍ، فَقُلْتُ: مَن هَؤُلَاءِ يَا جِبْرِيلُ؟ فقال: الخُطَبَاءُ مِن أُمَّتِك، يَأْمُرُونَ النَّاسَ بِالبِرِّ وَيَنْسَوْنَ أَنفُسَهم وهم يَتْلُونَ الكِتَابَ، أَفَلَا يَعْقِلُونَ؟ ».

When I was taken on the Night Journey I saw some men whose lips were being cut with scissors of fire, so I asked, "Who are they O Jibreel?" He said, "The preachers from your *Ummah* who order the people with righteousness, but leave it themselves, whilst they recite the Book - will they not understand?"[66]

This is one of the most important matters for the caller to Allaah, the One free of all imperfections, since it happens that you see a caller or a preacher speaking about abstaining from this world (*zuhd*) but his own state contradicts this. Or he speaks concerning backbiting whilst it is his practice, or he speaks about the Hereafter whereas it is the last thing on his mind and he does not prepare for it!

So one whose condition is like this, then we will fear for him, and there is great benefit in avoiding him unless one intends to advise or remind him! And from those matters which must be known is: the carefulness and precision of the caller.

---

66. Reported by Ibn Hibbaan (no.53 of *al-Ihsaan*). Its chain of narration is *hasan* if Allaah wills.

Hadeeth Twenty Eight
Carefulness and Precision of the Caller

From Aboo Hurairah (*radiyallaahu 'anhu*) who said that Allaah's Messenger (ﷺ) said:

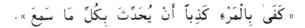

It is sufficient falsehood for a person that he narrates everything which he hears.[67]

The caller is careful in everything, particularly with regard to what he hears from the people, or what he reads in books. So it is an obligation upon him to carefully check and verify everything which reaches his ears or eyes before spreading it amongst the people and circulating it. His carefulness will be increased with regard to two cases:

1. When what is being conveyed to him is connected to the *Deen* and the *Sharee'ah*, such as something being quoted as a *hadeeth*, or a *fiqh* ruling and the like.
2. If someone reports something bad about a person, or an evil word from someone. He must check its correctness, carefully find out the reality and what is correct and not instead hasten to transmit it and add it to the stream of news! Carefulness will lead the caller to observe the value of ones time.

---

67. Reported by Muslim in the introduction of his *Saheeh* (no. 5), Aboo Daawood (no. 4971), Ibn Hibbaan (no. 30) and Al-Haakim (1/112). It's chain of narration is *saheeh*.

I have spoken about its chain of narration, despite it being reported in *Saheeh Muslim* since he reported in the introduction and the scholars differentiate between what he reports in his *Saheeh* and what he reports in its' introduction, as I have explained elsewhere, and success is granted by Allaah.

Hadeeth Twenty Nine
The Value of Ones' Time

From az-Zubayr ibn 'Adiyy *(radiyallaahu 'anhu)* who said:

دَخَلْنا على أَنَس بن مالك، فَشَكَوْنا إليه ما نَلْقَىٰ مِن الحَجَّاج،
فقال: « اصْبِروا، لا يَأْتِي عليكم زمانٌ إلاَّ بالّذي بعدَه شَرٌّ منه، حتى
تَلْقَوْا رَبَّكم » سمعتُ هذا مِن نَبِيّكم.

**We entered upon Anas ibn Maalik and complained to
him of what we suffered from al-Hajjaaj.[68] So he said,
"Have patience, a time will not come upon you except
that what comes after it is worse than it - until you meet
your Lord. I heard this from your Prophet."[69]**

Time is of the utmost value and this increases day by day, particularly since
the *hadeeth* contains a dire warning for all the *Ummah* if it does not utilize
and benefit from the time it has.

The value of time can be seen from what the scholars of *tafseer* say regarding
Soorah al-'Asr (no. 103), from them al-Fakhrur-Raazee who said in his *tafseer*
(32/84):

"Allaah, the Most High, swore an oath by time, due to the amazing things it
contains happiness and adversity, health and illness, and wealth and poverty
all occur in it, and nothing is equal to it in value. So if you were to waste a
thousand years uselessly, but then repent and success was confirmed for

---

68. He was ath-Thaqafee, and is well known. Adh-Dhahabee said in *Siyar A'laamin-Nubalaa* (4/
343) at the end of his biography: "We revile him and do not love him, rather we hate him for
Allaah. He had some good deeds, but they are drowned in the ocean of his sins, and his affair
is for Allaah!"

69. Reported by al-Bukhaaree (no.7068) [eng. trans. vol.9, p.151, no. 188].

you in the last moment of your life then you will remain in Paradise forever. The best of all things was your life at that moment. Time is one of the principle blessings, so Allaah swears an oath by it, and indicates that the day and the night is an opportunity which mankind wastes! And that the time is more excellent than the place - so He swears an oath by it - since time is a pure blessing containing no blemish, rather the one at loss and the blameworthy one is man!"

So he who recognises the value of time must realise that the hours of his life are either for him or against him, so it is to be said to him: seize the opportunity.

Hadeeth Thirty
Seize the Opportunity [70]

From Ibn 'Abbaas *(radiyallaahu 'anhuma)* who said that Allaah's Messenger (ﷺ) said to a man whilst advising him:

« اغْتَنِمْ خَمْساً قبل خَمْس، شبابَكَ قبل هَرَمك، وصِحَّتَكَ قبل سَقَمِك، وغَناءَك قبل فَقرك، وفراغَكَ قبل شُغْلك، وحياتَك قبل موتك. »

Take benefit of five before five: your youth before your old age, your health before your sickness, your wealth before your poverty, your free-time before you are preoccupied, and your life before your death.[71]

So these things, the benefit of which is to be seized, and which we have been ordered to make use of, all of them are signs of good, and indications of righteousness. But if one does not do so, then they turn against him, and it is to be said to him:

"Time is the most precious thing which you take care of,

And I see it to be the easiest for you to lose."[72]

---

70. See *al-Arba'oon-Fish-Shakhsiyyatil-Islaamiyyah* (no. 11) published by Daar Ibnil-Qayyim, Dammaam.

71. Reported by al-Haakim (4/306) and al-Baihaqee in *Shu'abul-Eemaan* (2/3/240) with a *saheeh* isnaad, and it was declared *hasan* by al-'Iraaqee in *Takhreejul-Ihyaa'*, (4/443). It is reported by Ibnul-Mubaarak in *az-Zuhd* (no. 2), and Aboo Nu'aym in *al-Kubraa* as occurs in *Tuhfatul-Ashraaf* (13/328), al-Qudaa'ee in *Musnadush-Shihaab* (no. 729), al-Khateeb in *'Iqtidaa-ul-'Ilm* (no. 170) and in *al-Faqeeh wal-Mutafaqqih* (2/87) - by way of 'Amr ibn Maymoon in *mursal* form with *hasan* isnaad.

72. *Dhayl-Tabaqaatil-Hanaabilah* (1/281).

This is so, since, "A person's time is actually his life, and it is the substance of his everlasting life in permanent bliss, or of having to suffer severe torment, and it passes swiftly like the passing of the clouds. So that of his time which is for Allaah and in obedience to Allaah then that is his lifespan, and other than that is not counted amongst his life. So if he lives in it like the animals, and spends his time in heedlessness and negligence, and futile desires and the best part of his time is when he sleeps or is inactive - then death is better for him than life."

Something else that must be known in order to be aware of it is the caller's trial.

Hadeeth Thirty One
The Caller's Trial (Affliction)

From Abul-A'war as-Sulamee *(radiyallaahu 'anhu)* who said that Allaah's Messenger (ﷺ) said:

« إِيَّاكَ وأبوابُ السُّلطانِ، فإِنَّه قد أَصْبَحَ صَعْباً هَبوطاً ».

Avoid the gates of the Ruler, since it becomes hard to endure and is degrading. [73]

Drawing near to the Ruler is one of the greatest trials and it exposes one to very great affliction. "One of the greatest of things to be feared for one who enters upon the unjust Rulers is that he will agree with their falsehood, and help them in their injustice even if only by remaining silent and not admonishing them. Indeed one who by his entering upon them wishes for eminence and leadership and craves after this, then he will not admonish them. Rather he will perhaps make some of their evil deeds seem alluring to them in order to gain their favour and improve his own standing with them and that they may help him to attain his goals."[74]

From the great affliction is that Shaitaan may make drawing near to the Ruler seem attractive to the caller by suggesting that it will be beneficial for *da'wah*, and good for the *Deen* but this is not the case at all with him! Rather it is for his own personal gain, and to keep his own position and status!

---

73. Reported by Ibnul 'Asaakir (12/q. 462 of my copy) by way of 'Ubayd ibn Ya'eesh: Muhammad ibn Fudayl narrated to us, from Ismaa'eel, from Qays, from him. It is reported by at-Tabaraanee in *al Awsat* as occurs in *al-Majma'* (5/246) and al-Haithumee said: "It's narrators are those of the *Saheeh*."

Its *isnaad* is *hasan* as it contains Ibn Fudayl. The name of Abul-A'war as-Sulamee is 'Amr ibn Sufyaan and his being a Companion is affirmed by a number of the scholars. [See *al-Istighnaa' fil-Kunaa'*(1/103) of Ibn 'Abdul-Barr].

74. *Sharh Hadeeth maa dhibaan jaai'aan* (p.50) of Ibn Rajab.

Approaching the ruler, if it is indeed done to give *da'wah* to him and to order him with the good and to forbid him from evil, then it is a good action for which he will receive an excellent reward from his Lord, since: the callers proclaiming the truth is one of the most important matters.

Hadeeth Thirty Two
The Callers Proclaiming the Truth

From 'Alee *(radiyallaahu 'anhu)* **who said:**

لَمَّا ضَمَمْتُ إِلَيَّ سلاحَ رسولِ اللهِ ﷺ ، وجدتُ في قائمِ سيفِ رسولِ اللهِ ﷺ رقْعَةً فيها :

« صِلْ مَن قَطَعَكَ ، وأَحْسِنْ إلى مَن أَساءَ إليك ، وقُلِ الحقَّ ولو على نَفْسِك . »

When I took possession of the weapons of Allaah's Messenger (ﷺ) I found in the hilt of his sword a parchment saying, "Keep relations with those who cut off from you, and behave well towards one who treats you badly, and speak the truth even if it is against yourself."[75]

These are from the important matters which must be remembered and reminder given concerning them, particularly in this time when peoples' concepts have become confused, and they disagree about principles, and mutual flattery has taken the place of advising and reminding.

But the caller must proclaim the truth in a good manner as has preceded, without differentiating between Ruler or ruled, shaikh or follower, himself or someone else. And his proclaiming the truth necessitates that he defend the believers.

---

75. Reported by Aboo 'Amr ibnus-Sammaak in his *Hadeeth* (2/28/1) as occurs in *as-Saheehah* (no. 1911), and Ibnun-Najjaar in *Dhaylut-Taareekh* as occurs in *Jam'ul-Jawaami'* (no. 6929 of my numbering), by way of Ibraaheem ibn al-Mundhir, from: Husayn ibn Zayd, from Ja'far ibn Muhammad, from his father, from his grandfather, from 'Alee. Its *isnaad* is *hasan*, both Ibraaheem and Husayn are of the level of *sadooq* (truthful).

Hadeeth Thirty Three
Defending the Believers

From Sa'eed ibn al-Musayyib (*rahimahullaah*) who said:

بينما رسولُ اللهِ ﷺ جالسٌ ومعه أصحابُه، وَقَعَ رَجُلٌ بأبي بكرٍ.
فآذاه، فَصَمَتَ عنه أبو بكرٍ، ثُمَّ آذاهُ الثانيةَ، فَصَمَتَ عنه أبو بكرٍ، ثُمَّ
آذاهُ الثالثةَ، فانْتَصَرَ منه أبو بكرٍ، فقام رسولُ اللهِ ﷺ حين انْتَصَرَ
أبو بكرٍ، فقال أبو بكرٍ: أَوَجَدْتَ عَلَيَّ يا رسولَ اللهِ؟ فقال رسولُ
اللهِ ﷺ:

« نَزَلَ مَلَكٌ مِنَ السَّمَاءِ يُكَذِّبُهُ بِمَا قَالَ لَكَ، فَلَمَّا انْتَصَرْتَ، وَقَعَ
الشَّيْطَانُ. فلم أَكُنْ لأَجْلِسَ إذ وَقَعَ الشَّيْطَانُ » .

**Whilst Allaah's Messenger (ﷺ) was sitting with his
Companions, a man reviled Aboo Bakr and offended
him but Aboo Bakr remained silent, then he offended
him for a second time and Aboo Bakr remained silent,
then he offended him for a third time so Aboo Bakr
avenged himself. Allaah's Messenger (ﷺ) stood up when
Aboo Bakr took revenge, so Aboo Bakr asked, "Are
you annoyed with me O Messenger of Allaah?" Allaah's
Messenger (ﷺ) said, "An Angel descended from the
heavens declaring him a liar in what he said to you, but
when you took revenge Shaitaan came, and I was not
going to remain seated when the Shaitaan came."[76]**

So defending the Muslims is a very great deed, through it the caller preserves
the rope of love between himself and his brothers those whom he knows

---

76. Reported by Aboo Daawood (no. 4896) [eng. trans. vol. 3, p.1364, no. 4878] and al-Bukhaaree
in his *Taareekhul-Kabeer*'(2/102). Its *isnaad* is of the level of *hasan*.

and those he does not. But if, instead, he remains silent and does not speak, and prefers silence to assisting and defending his brothers then he has acted contrary to the order of the Messenger (ﷺ) who said:

Help your brother whether he is an oppressor or one who is oppressed.[77]

As is clear that when a Muslim defends his Muslim brother from the tongues of those who backbite or defame him, then that will be a very great help. In addition to suppressing Shaitaan and his plans, correcting himself and his brother, and in lessening the seeds of evil and corruption between the people, it elevates the *da'wah* and gives it due respect.

What I have indicated points to a further important matter which is: The caller's environment.

---

77. Reported by al-Bukhaaree [eng. trans. vol.3, p.373, no. 623) from the *hadeeth* of Anas, a further narration from him (no. 624) is: Anas (*radiyallaahu 'anhu*) said that Allaah's Messenger (ﷺ) said, "Help your brother whether he is an oppressor, or one who is oppressed." They said, "We will help him if he is oppressed, but how should we help him if he is an oppressor?" He said: "Prevent him from it." [Translator's note]

Hadeeth Thirty Four
The Caller's Environment

From Aboo Sa'eed al-Khudree *(radiyallaahu 'anhu)* who said that
Allaah's Messenger (ﷺ) said:

« كان في بَني إسرائيلَ رَجُلٌ قَتَلَ تِسْعَةً وتِسْعِينَ إنساناً، ثُمَّ خَرَجَ
يَسْأَلُ، فَأَتَى راهِباً فَسَأَلَهُ، فقال له: أَلِي تَوْبَةٌ؟ قال: لا، فَقَتَلَهُ، فَجَعَلَ
يَسْأَلُ؟ فقال له رَجُلٌ: إِنْتِ قَرْيَةَ كَذَا وكَذَا، فَأَدْرَكَهُ المَوْتُ، فَنَأَى
بِصَدْرِهِ نَحْوَهَا، فاخْتَصَمَت فيه ملائِكَةُ الرَّحْمَةِ، وملائِكَةُ العَذَابِ،
فَأَوْحَى اللهُ إلى هٰذه: أَنْ تَقَرَّبي، وأَوْحى اللهُ إلى هٰذه: أَنْ تَبَاعَدي،
وقال: قِيسُوا ما بَيْنَهُما، فَوَجَداه إلى هٰذه أَقْرَبَ بِشِبْرٍ، فَغُفِرَ له ».

**There was amongst the children of Israa'eel a man who
killed ninety-nine people, then he went out enquiring,
so he came to a monk and asked him, "Is there any
repentance for me?" He (the monk) said, "No." So he
killed him. Then he again continued asking, so a man
said to him, "Go to such and such a town," but death
overtook him (on the way) but while dying he turned
his chest to that village. So the angels of mercy and the
angels of punishment disputed concerning him. So
Allaah ordered the (village where he was going) to draw
nearer to him and Allaah ordered the other to move
further away, and said, "Measure what is between him
and them." So they found him closer to the one (he
was going to) by one span, so he was forgiven.[78]**

---

78. Reported by al-Bukhaaree [eng. trans. vol.4, p.450, no. 676] and Muslim [eng. trans. vol.4, p.
1443, no. 6662 & 6663].

Imaam Muslim's wording:

'There was amongst those who came before you a man who killed ninety nine people. Then he

63

The caller's correcting his environment has very great importance, particularly if he has just started upon the right way and just begun his *da'wah*.[79] However, if he is not able to do that then he must move from that environment which is one of weakness, evil and sin to one where goodness and piety are predominant. The *hadeeth* mentioned here is a strong proof for what we have mentioned, "since it shows that the person who repents should leave the environment which he was used to when he was upon sin, and to leave all of that and preoccupy himself with other than it."[80]

From those things which must be known is the methodology of the caller.

---

asked about the most knowledgeable person upon the earth, so he was directed to a monk. He came to him and said that he had killed ninety nine people and asked was there any repentance for him. So he (the monk) replied, "No." So he killed him and completed a hundred. Then he asked about the most knowledgeable person upon the earth, so he was directed to a scholar. He told him (the scholar) that he had killed a hundred people, and was there any repentance for him? So he (the scholar) said, "Yes and who can stand between you and repentance! Go to such and such land where there are people who worship Allaah, so worship Allaah along with them and do not return to your land because it is a land of evil." So he set off until he reached half way when death came upon him. So the angels of mercy and the angels of punishment disputed about him. The angels of mercy said, "He came in repentance turning to Allaah with his heart," and the angels of punishment said, "He never performed any good." So an angel came to them in the form of a human and they made him a judge between them.* So he said, "Measure his distance from the two lands, so whichever you find him closest to then he is for that." So they measured and found him closest to the land where he intended to go - thus the angels of mercy took him.'

* This has to be understood to be something Allaah ordered them to do as explained by an-Nawawee in his *Sharh* (17/84) [Translator's note].

79. See *hadeeth* no. 20.

80. *Fathul-Baaree* (6/517-518).

Hadeeth Thirty Five
The Methodology of the Caller

From Aboo Tufayl 'Aamir ibn Waathilah (radiyallaahu 'anhu) who said:

كنتُ عند عليِّ بن أبي طالبٍ، فأتاه رَجُلٌ، فقالَ: ما كان
النبيُّ ﷺ يُسِرُّ إليكَ؟! قال: فَغَضِبَ وقال: ما كان النبيُّ ﷺ يُسِرُّ إليَّ
شَيئاً يَكتُمُهُ النَّاسَ، غَيرَ أنَّه حَدَّثَني بكلماتٍ أُربَعٍ، قَالَ: فقالَ: ما هُنَّ
يا أميرَ المُؤمِنينَ؟ قالَ: قالَ:

« لَعَنَ اللهُ مَن لَعَنَ والِدَهُ، ولَعَنَ اللهُ مَن ذَبَحَ لِغَيرِ اللهِ، ولَعَنَ اللهُ
مَن آوىٰ مُحْدِثاً، ولَعَنَ اللهُ مَن غَيَّرَ مَنَارَ الأَرْضِ ».

I was with 'Alee ibn Abee Taalib (radiyallaahu 'anhu) when a man came to him and asked, "What private information did the Prophet (ﷺ) give to you?" So he became angry and said, "The Prophet (ﷺ) had not used to tell me anything privately which he hid from the people, but he did tell me four things." So he enquired, "What are they O Chief of Believers?" He replied, "He said: may Allaah's curse be upon the one who curses his father, may Allaah's curse be upon one who sacrifices for other than Allaah, may Allaah's curse be upon one who accommodates an innovator/evildoer, and may Allaah's curse be upon one who tampers with boundary posts of the land."[81]

This hadeeth, despite the small number of its sentences and the briefness of its wording, explains to the caller the principles of his methodology, the

---

81. Reported by Muslim in his Saheeh (no. 1978) [eng. trans. vol.3, p. 1093, no. 4876].

pillars of his *da'wah*, and the rights upon which the *Deen* is built.

The first point affirms personal rights; the second point affirms the rights of *Tawheed*; the third point affirms the rights of worship (*'Ibaadah*); and the fourth point affirms the rights of others.

So whoever looks after the rights of his own self, safeguards the *Tawheed* of Allaah, upholds the rights of worship, and fulfils the rights of others - then his methodology will be complete, and his conduct good. Reminding others of these four comprehensive matters, and calling to them is not an easy affair as some people expect or imagine, rather it is something difficult which will occupy the greater part of the caller's life and still he will not be able to fully satisfy all that it demands.

Thus whoever removes himself from this clear methodology in *da'wah* comprising of these affairs, turning his attention instead to foolish matters and superficial things, then he must re-examine and reconsider his affair. And this will necessitate understanding the caller's wisdom.

Hadeeth Thirty Six
The Wisdom of the Caller

From Aboo Hurairah (*radiyallaahu 'anhu*) who said that Allaah's Messenger (ﷺ) said:

$$\text{« لا يُلْدَغُ الْمُؤْمِنُ مِن جُحْرٍ واحِدٍ مَرَّتَيْنِ »}$$

The Believer is not stung from the same hole twice.[82]

So if he was involved in something, then comes to know after a long time that it is not beneficial and correct, then does he remain upon that and continue in it?! If he does this then he will indeed be far from having wisdom, but if he takes heed and turns away from it then that is due to a high level of *eemaan* and wisdom.

This *hadeeth* "is an example given by the Prophet (ﷺ) to show the complete caution and alertness of the Believer, and that the Believer is prevented by his *eemaan* from committing sins which will indeed harm him and that when he falls into any of them then he immediately regrets it, repents and turns back (to Allaah). From the completeness of his repentance is that he is very careful to avoid that which caused him to fall into the sin just like one who entered his hand into a hole and was bitten by a snake, he is hardly likely to enter his hand in that hole again due to what happened the first time he did so."[83]

The caller in this regard should be as Ibn Mas'ood (*radiyallaahu 'anhu*) said:

"The fortunate one is he who *takes lesson from the (fate) of others.*"[84]

---

82. Reported by al-Bukhaaree (10/529) [eng.trans. vol.8, p.97, no. 154] and Muslim (no.2997) [eng. trans. vol.4, p.1541, no. 7137].

83. *Bahjatul-Abraar* (p.227).

84. Reported from him by Muslim (no.2645) [eng. trans. vol.4, p.1392, no. 6393)].

So how about one whose own soul admonishes him, yet he does not take heed of the admonition! And from those things which increase his wisdom are the trials faced by the caller.

Hadeeth Thirty Seven
Trials Faced by the Believer

From Khabbaab ibnul Aratt (*radiyallaahu 'anhu*) who said:

شَكَوْنَا إلى رسولِ الله ﷺ وهومُتَوَسِّدٌ بُرْدَةً له في ظِلِّ الكعبةِ، قُلنا له: أَلا تَسْتَنْصِرُ؟ أَلاَ تدعو اللهَ لنا؟ قال:

« كان الرَّجُلُ فيمنْ قَبْلَكم يُحْفَرُ له في الأرض ِ، فَيُجْعَلُ فيه، فَيُجَاءُ بالمِنْشَار، فَيُوضَعُ على رأسِهِ فَيُشَقُّ باثْنَتَيْن، وما يَصُدُّهُ ذلك عن دينِه، ويُمْشَطُ بأمشَاطِ الحديد ما دونَ لَحْمِه مِن عَظْمٍ أو عَصَبٍ، وما يَصُدُّهُ ذلك عن دينِه، واللهِ لَيُتِمَّنَّ هذا الأَمْرَ حَتَّى يَسِيرَ الرَّاكِبُ مِن صَنْعَاءَ إلى حَضْرَمَوْتَ لا يَخافُ إلاَّ اللهَ، أو الذِّئْبَ على غَنَمِهِ، وَلكِنَّكُمْ تَسْتَعْجِلونَ » .

We complained to Allaah's Messenger (ﷺ) (of the persecution of the pagans) whilst he was sitting in the shade of the Ka'bah leaning upon his cloak. We said to him, "Will you not seek help for us? Would you call upon Allaah for us?" He replied, "Amongst those before you a (believing) man would have a hole dug for him, and he would be placed in it. Then a saw would be brought and placed upon his head and it would be sawn in half, yet that would not make him abandon his religion, and his body would be torn with iron combs, the flesh from his bones and nerves being removed - yet that would not make him give up his religion. By Allaah this *Deen* will prevail till a rider will travel from San'aa to Hadramaut not fearing except Allaah, and the wolf as regards his sheep, but you (people) are impatient."[85]

---

85. Reported by al-Bukhaaree in his *Saheeh* [eng. trans. vol. 4, p.519, no.809).

So through this (i.e. trials) the strong are sorted from the weak, the intelligent from the feeble minded, as Allaah, the One free of all imperfections, says:

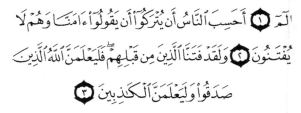

"Alif Laam Meem. Do people think that they will be left alone because they say 'We believe,' and will not be tested. And we indeed tested those who were before them. And Allaah will certainly make (it) known (the truth of) those who are true, and will certainly make (it) known (the falsehood of) those who are liars, (although Allaah knows all that before putting them to test)."[86]

Trials only improve the caller and do not demean him, and they benefit him with Allaah and do not harm him, and it is something that must occur to one who loves Allaah and His Messenger, as the Prophet (ﷺ) said:

"Trials come more quickly to one who loves me than the torrent surges to its end."[87]

These trials are the *Sunnah* of Allaah, the One free of all imperfections, with regard to the prophets, the pious, and the callers throughout the ages, and there are many stories in the Noble Book and the Pure *Sunnah* which make this clear and emphasise it.

So to remain firm in giving *da'wah* and to bear the trials patiently we must concentrate upon quality, not quantity.

---

86. Soorah al-'Ankaboot (29):1-3

87. Reported by Ibn Hibbaan (no. 2911) with a *hasan* chain of narration.

Hadeeth Thirty Eight
Quality not Quantity

From Thawbaan (*radiyallaahu 'anhu*) who said that Allaah's Messenger (ﷺ) said:

« يُوشِكُ الأَمَمُ أَنْ تَـداعَـى عَلَيْكُمْ، كَما تَـداعَـى الأَكَلَـةُ عَلـى قَصْعَتِها » .

فقال قائلٌ: ومِن قِلَّةٍ نحنُ يومئذٍ؟ قال:

« بل أنتم يومئذٍ كثيرٌ! ولكنكم غُثاءٌ كَغُثاءِ السَّيْلِ، وَلَيَنْزِعَنَّ اللهُ مِن صُدورِ عَدُوِّكُمُ المهابَةَ مِنكم، وَلَيَقْذِفَنَّ اللهُ في قلوبِكم الوَهَنَ » .

فقال قائلٌ: يا رسولَ الله! وما الوَهَنُ؟ قال:

« حُبُّ الدُّنيا وكراهيةُ المَوْت » .

"The nations are about to invite one another and come upon you just as those eating invite others to share in their dish." Someone asked, "Will that be because we are few in number that day?" He replied, "No, at that time you will be numerous! But you will be froth/scum like the froth/scum carried by the torrent, and Allaah will remove the fear of you from the hearts of your enemies, and Allaah will indeed throw weakness (*wahn*) into your hearts." So someone asked, "What is the weakness (*wahn*)?" He replied, "Love for the world and hatred for death."[88]

---

88. Reported by Aboo Daawood (no. 4297) [eng. trans. vol.3, p.1196, no. 4284] and ar-Ruwayaanee in his *Musnad* (q.134b.). *Hasan* due to supports reported by Ahmad (5/278), Aboo Nu'aim (1/182) and at-Tabaraanee in *al-Kabeer* (no. 1452).

If we gave importance to numbers and quantity then the scum would be better off than us. Large numbers without sense, understanding and education will certainly cause harm and it is certainly something dangerous since it produces a false impression of correctness, then failure to accept the truth, then disagreement and disunity... then frustration and defeat. Perhaps this was what the Prophet (ﷺ) indicated by his saying:

"...and twelve thousand will not be defeated due to lack of numbers."[89]

The number that we have is not small, rather it is many - then why is this great number defeated? It is defeated because it does not give importance to the main principle of Islaam which is the *Tawheed* of Allaah, the Blessed and Most High, and because it does not educate the callers to recognise rights and carry out the obligations, so they become weak and feeble, so they become the tail of the convoy after being its head, and they become weak after being strong.

If only the caller received the true education and training, and proceeded upon the way and methodology of the Prophet (ﷺ) then without a doubt he would reach the highest goal.

---

89. The *hadeeth* is *hasan* and I have quoted it fully with the details of its sources in *Juz Luwayn* (no. 8) - may Allaah make its completion easy.

Reported by Ahmad, Aboo Daawood, at-Tirmidhee and others as occurs in *as-Saheehah* (no. 986) [Translator's note].

Hadeeth Thirty Nine
The Callers Highest Goal

From a man of the Companions of the Prophet (ﷺ) who said that the Prophet (ﷺ) said:

« لَنْ يَهْلِكَ النَّاسُ حَتَّى يُعْذَرُوا مِنْ أَنْفُسِهِمْ ».

The people will not perish until they have no excuse left for themselves.[90]

This is what Allaah wishes from us - that we proceed upon the correct methodology (*manhaj*), and if we reach honour, ascendancy and victory, then it is from the blessings and favours of Allaah, and if not then we excuse ourselves before Allaah, the One free of all imperfections, that we carried out the obligation due upon us.

Therefore it is not upon Allaah, the Majestic, that He should give us victory over our enemies in our lifetime, no - rather the obligation that we have carried out may be a step for future victory which may come at the hands of our children or those after them. In Islamic history lies a great lesson, and from this is the saying of Allaah, the One free of all imperfections, to his Prophet (ﷺ):

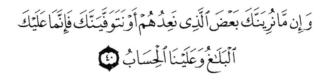

وَإِن مَّا نُرِيَنَّكَ بَعْضَ ٱلَّذِى نَعِدُهُمْ أَوْ نَتَوَفَّيَنَّكَ فَإِنَّمَا عَلَيْكَ ٱلْبَلَٰغُ وَعَلَيْنَا ٱلْحِسَابُ ۝

"Whether We show you (O Muhammad (ﷺ)) part of what We have promised them or cause you to die,

---

90. Reported by Ahmad (5/292), Aboo Daawood (no. 4347) and Ibnul-Ja'd in his *Musnad* (no. 130) by various chains from Shu'bah, from 'Amr ibn Murrah, from Abul-Bukhtaree who said: "I was informed by one who heard the Prophet (ﷺ)." I say: This *isnaad* is *saheeh*.

your duty is only to convey (the Message) and unto Us is the reckoning."[91]

This is a very great lesson for the callers to Allaah, the One free of all imperfections and the Most High, so that they are aware what is for them and what is against them, so that they may repent to their Lord and return to the methodology of their Prophet (ﷺ), and say with full conviction: We are Muslims and that is enough.

---

91. Soorah ar-Ra'd (13):40

Hadeeth Forty
We are Muslims and that is Enough

From al-Haarith al-Ash'aree (*radiyallaahu 'anhu*) who said that
Allaah's Messenger (ﷺ) said:

« إِنَّ اللهَ تَعَالَى أَمَرَ يَحْيَى بْنَ زَكَرِيَّا عَلَيْهِمَا السَّلَامُ بِخَمْسِ كَلِمَاتٍ،
يَعْمَلُ بِهِنَّ، وَيَأْمُرُ بَنِي إِسْرَائِيلَ يَعْمَلُونَ بِهِنَّ، وَأَنَّ عِيسَى بْنَ مَرْيَمَ
عَلَيْهِ السَّلَامُ قَالَ لَهُ: إِنَّ اللهَ (أَمَرَكَ) بِخَمْسِ كَلِمَاتٍ، تَعْمَلُ بِهِنَّ،
وَتَأْمُرُ بِهِنَّ بَنِي إِسْرَائِيلَ يَعْمَلُونَ بِهِنَّ، فَإِمَّا أَنْ تَأْمُرَهُمْ وَإِمَّا أَنْ
آمُرَهُمْ، قَالَ: إِنَّكَ إِنْ تَسْبِقْنِي بِهِنَّ خَشِيتُ أَنْ أُعَذَّبَ أَوْ يُخْسَفَ بِي،
قَالَ: فَجَمَعَ النَّاسَ فِي بَيْتِ المَقْدِسِ، حَتَّى امْتَلَأَ، وَقَعَدَ النَّاسُ عَلَى
الشُّرُفَاتِ، قَالَ: فَوَعَظَهُمْ، قَالَ: إِنَّ اللهَ أَمَرَنِي بِخَمْسِ كَلِمَاتٍ، أَعْمَلُ
بِهِنَّ، وَآمُرُكُمْ أَنْ تَعْمَلُوا بِهِنَّ، أَوَّلُهُنَّ: أَنْ تَعْبُدُوا اللهَ، وَلَا تُشْرِكُوا بِهِ
شَيْئاً، وَأَنَّ مَثَلَ مَنْ أَشْرَكَ بِاللهِ كَمَثَلِ رَجُلٍ اشْتَرَى عَبْداً مِنْ خَالِصِ
مَالِهِ بِذَهَبٍ أَوْ وَرِقٍ، قَالَ: هَذِهِ دَارِي، وَهَذَا عَمَلِي، فَاعْمَلْ وَأَدِّ إِلَيَّ،
فَجَعَلَ يَعْمَلُ وَيُؤَدِّي إِلَى غَيْرِ سَيِّدِهِ، فَأَيُّكُمْ يَسُرُّهُ أَنْ يَكُونَ عَبْدُهُ
كَذَلِكَ؟ فَإِنَّ اللهَ خَلَقَكُمْ وَرَزَقَكُمْ، فَلَا تُشْرِكُوا بِهِ شَيْئاً، وَآمُرُكُمْ
بِالصَّلَاةِ، فَإِذَا صَلَّيْتُمْ فَلَا تَلْتَفِتُوا، وَآمُرُكُمْ بِالصِّيَامِ، وَأَنَّ مَثَلَ ذَلِكَ
كَمَثَلِ رَجُلٍ كَانَتْ مَعَهُ صُرَّةٌ فِيهَا مِسْكٌ، وَمَعَهُ عِصَابَةٌ، كُلُّهُمْ يُعْجِبُهُمْ
أَنْ يَجِدَ رِيحَهَا، فَإِنَّ الصَّائِمَ عِنْدَ اللهِ، يَعْنِي أَطْيَبُ مِنْ رِيحِ المِسْكِ،
وَآمُرُكُمْ بِالصَّدَقَةِ، فَإِنَّ مَثَلَ ذَلِكَ كَمَثَلِ رَجُلٍ أَسَرَهُ العَدُوُّ، وَقَامُوا إِلَيْهِ
فَأَوْثَقُوا يَدَهُ إِلَى عُنُقِهِ، فَقَالَ: هَلْ لَكُمْ أَنْ أَفْدِيَ نَفْسِي مِنْكُمْ؟ قَالَ:
فَجَعَلَ يُعْطِيهِمُ القَلِيلَ وَالكَثِيرَ لِيَفُكَّ نَفْسَهُ مِنْهُمْ، وَآمُرُكُمْ بِذِكْرِ اللهِ
كَثِيراً، وَأَنَّ مَثَلَ ذَلِكَ كَمَثَلِ رَجُلٍ طَلَبَهُ العَدُوُّ سِرَاعاً فِي أَثَرِهِ، حَتَّى
أَتَى عَلَى حِصْنٍ حَصِينٍ فَأَحْرَزَ نَفْسَهُ فِيهِ، كَذَلِكَ العَبْدُ لَا يُحْرِزُ نَفْسَهُ
مِنَ الشَّيْطَانِ إِلَّا بِذِكْرِ اللهِ عَزَّ وَجَلَّ ».

وقَالَ رَسُولُ اللهِ ﷺ :

« وَأنا آمُرُكُمْ بِخَمسٍ أمَرَني اللهُ بِهِنَّ: الجَماعَةِ، وَالسَّمعِ، وَالطَّاعَةِ، وَالهِجْرَةِ، وَالجِهَادِ في سبيلِ اللهِ عزَّ وَجَلَّ، فَمَنْ فارَقَ الجَماعَةَ قَيْدَ شِبْرٍ خَلَعَ، يَعْني رِبْقَةَ الأسْلامِ مِن رَأسِهِ، إلاَّ أنْ يَرْجِعَ، وَمَنْ دَعَا بِدَعْوَى الجَاهِلِيَّةِ فَإنَّهُ مِن جُثا جَهَنَّمَ ».

قِيلَ: وَإنْ صَامَ وَصَلَّى؟ قَالَ:

« وَإنْ صَامَ وَصَلَّى، فَادعوا بِدَعْوَى اللهِ الّذي سَمَّى اللهُ بِهِ: المُسْلِمينَ، المُؤمِنينَ، عِبَادَ اللهِ ».

Indeed Allaah, the Most High, ordered Yahyaa ibn Zakariyyaa ('alaihimas salaam) with five things - that he should act upon them and order the Children of Israa'eel to act upon them. 'Eesaa ibn Maryam ('alaihis salaam) said to him (Zakariyyaa), "Indeed Allaah (ordered you) with five things, that you act upon them and that you order the children of Israa'eel to act upon them. So either you order them or I order them." So he (Zakariyyah) said, "If you precede me in that, I fear that I will be punished or swallowed by the earth." He said, "So he gathered the people in the (mosque) of Jerusalem until it was filled, and the people sat upon its walls." He said, "He admonished them saying: Indeed Allaah has ordered me with five things which I should act upon and order you to act upon. The first of them is that you worship Allaah and do not associate anything along with Him. That one who associates anything in worship with Allaah is like a man who bought a slave with his own wealth - either gold or silver, and said, 'This is my house and this is my work, so work and give the

76

wages to me,' but he pays the wages to other than his owner, then which of you would be pleased for his slave to be like that? But Allaah created you and provides for you, so do not associate anything in worship with Him. And I order you with the prayer and when you pray then do not turn aside. And I order you with fasting and that it is the like of a man who had a small pouch containing musk, amongst a group of people - all of them like to smell it - the fasting person to Allaah is better than the smell of musk. And I order you with *sadaqah* (charity) - for its likeness is that of a man taken prisoner by the enemy, so they take hold of him and tie his hand to his neck,[92] so he says, 'Will you allow me to ransom myself from you?'" He said, "So he gives them small and large amounts[93] to escape from them. And I order you to make mention of Allaah much, and the like of that is a man being chased by the enemy who are hastening after him until he comes to a protected fortress and so protects himself in it, likewise is the servant, for he does not protect himself from the Shaitaan except through remembrance of Allaah, the Mighty and Majestic."

Allaah's Messenger (ﷺ) said, "I order you with five things which Allaah ordered me with: The *jamaa'ah*,[94]

---

92. In the narration of Tirmidhee he adds, "so they bring him forward to strike his neck ...". [Translator's note]

93. i.e. whatever he has [Translator's note]

94. At-Teebee said, "What is meant by the *Jamaa'ah* is the Companions and the Taabi'een, and the generation after the Taabi'een - the Pious Predecessors: That is, I order you to cling to their guidance and their way and to associate with them." (*Tuhfatul-Ahwadhee Sharh Sunanut-Tirmidhee* (8/162)). [Translator's note]

hearing, obeying, *hijrah*, and *jihaad* in the way of Allaah, the Mighty and Majestic. So whoever separates from the *jamaa'ah* by a handspan throws off the yoke of Islaam from his neck unless he repents/returns, and whoever calls with the calls of the days of ignorance then he is from the horde of Hell-Fire." It was said, "Even if he fasts and prays?" He said, "Even if he fasts and prays, so call with the call of Allaah, which Allaah gave: The Muslims, the Believers, Worshippers of Allaah."[95]

This *hadeeth* "comprehends all types of knowledge"[96] and the most important matter that we wish to draw attention to here is it's end: So call with the call of Allaah which Allaah gave: The Muslims, the Believers, Worshippers of Allaah.

Shaikhul-Islaam Ibn Taimiyyah[97] reports that one of the Salaf (Pious Predecessors) said, "I do not mind which out of the two blessings was greater, that Allaah guided me to Islaam, or that he kept me away from these innovated sects. By Allaah, the Most High, in the Qur'aan He called us the Muslims, the Believers and the Worshippers of Allaah, so we will not leave the names which Allaah has named us with in favour of names innovated by the people, which they call themselves by and also their forefathers for which Allaah has sent down no proof."

---

95. Reported by at-Tayaalisee (no.1161 and 1162), Ahmad (4/130, 202 and 344), at-Tirmidhee (no. 2863 and 2864), Ibn Khuzaimah (no. 1895), Aboo Ya'laa in his *Musnad* (no. 1571) and in *al-Mafaareed* (no. 83), and an-Nasaa'ee in *al-Kubraa* as occurs in *Tuhfatul-Ashraaf* (3/3) and *al-Arba'eenul-Jihaadiyyah* (no. 6) of Ibn 'Asaakir through two chains from Zayd ibn Sallaam, from Aboo Sallaam, from him. And its chain of narration is *saheeh*.

96. *Al-Istee'aab* (2/227) of Ibn 'Abdul-Barr.

97. In *al-Wasiyyatul-Kubraa* (p.76 of my checked version).

So if we are aware of this and it is fully comprehended by our minds, then our Islaam will return to its original purity and the call to Allaah, the One free of all imperfections, will become a lofty means to the end, not an end in itself. For indeed da'wah is a means to establish the worship of Allaah alone, the One free of all imperfections, and to single Him out with Tawheed. As He, the Most Mighty, says:

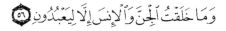

"I did not create jinn or mankind except to worship Me."[98]

And this is a very important matter for the one proceeding towards Allaah - the Most Perfect - but it is often misunderstood by those who have not received and learned the knowledge from its original sources - so with this person the affairs are turned upside down - so that the means become goals, and the goals become means! There is no power except by the will of Allaah.

---

98. Soorah adh-Dhaariyaat (51):56

Epilogue

Calling to Allaah, the One free of all imperfections, is a very great honour which is not reached through ease, repose and love of relaxation. It is reached through beneficial knowledge; righteous and correct action; careful following;[99] and through deep understanding. All this is to be accompanied by tenderness and mildness when giving admonition.

What I have written is a mere drop from an ocean, and it is not but a reminder - for myself firstly, then for my brothers, then for the whole Ummah.

So if I have spoken correctly, then it is from Allaah alone, and if I have made any error then it is from myself and from the Shaitaan. I ask for Allaah's forgiveness at the beginning and the end, outwardly and inwardly, and our final call is that all praise and thanks are due to Allaah, Lord of the worlds.

---

99. i.e. the *Sunnah* in the manner it was followed by the Pious Predecessors. [Translator's note].